CLERGY⊕KILLERS

Guidance for
Pastors and
Congregations
Under Attack

CLERGY KILLERS

Guidance for Pastors and Congregations Under Attack

G. LLOYD REDIGER

Logos Productions Inc.
Inver Grove Heights, MN

Cover and Text Design: Koechel Peterson & Associates, Minneapolis, MN

ISBN 1-885361-03-3

The paper used in this publication meets the minimum requirements of American National Standard for Information Sciences—Permanence of Paper for Printed Library Materials. ANSI Z329.48-1984.

Manufactured by Bolger Publications/Creative Printing
Printed in the United States of America

D E D I C A T I O N

I am greatly indebted to several persons who deserve to be named here, even though this is an inadequate expression of appreciation. First, I express my thanks to the hundreds of clergy and their intimates who have trusted me with their stories and their successes in confronting the abuse of clergy killers. In fact, I dedicate this book to the thousands of clergy who have suffered anonymously and publicly without the support they deserved.

Further, it is not just love and dutiful praise that cause me to express appreciation next for my spouse, Vera Marie. She is a soulmate as well as a tireless partner in the hard work required to produce a book like this.

My deep appreciation also goes to Beth Ann Gaede, who has an extraordinary talent for finding errors and offering valuable solutions as she edits a manuscript.

And finally, my sincere appreciation is offered to my associates at Logos Productions Inc., who have guided this book to completion. All these and many more dedicated servants of God care deeply about abused pastors and are doing what they can to heal this sickness in the church.

I trust it will not seem irreverent to express public and worshipful tribute to God in this mission. Seldom in my life and professional career have I felt so impelled and guided by God's Holy Spirit as I have since writing the first column entitled "Clergy Killers" which was published in the August 1993 issue of *The Clergy Journal*. This book grew out of the enormous outcry of suppressed pain and expectations uncovered by that column and many subsequent seminars across the nation. But the sensitivity of this subject has required me to rely heavily on God's guidance. This book is offered with a continuing prayer that it may accomplish the purposes for which God intends it.

CONTENTS

INTRODUCTION

A buse of pastors by congregations and the breakdown of pastors due to inadequate support are now
tragic realities. This worst-case scenario for the church,
one that is increasing in epidemic proportions, is not a
misinterpretation by a few discontented clergy. Rather,
it is a phenomenon that is verified by both research and
experience.

Worse yet, there is a strong tendency toward denial
of this reality in denominational offices and among
clergy who have not yet been forced out of their congregations or battered emotionally and spiritually
while trying to be faithful pastors.

It is hard to believe this is happening; the church, synagogue, and temple are the last places such behavior
would be expected. Even though there is abuse and violence in society, it seems incongruous that it would
happen in church. The church buildings and denominational offices still look much as they have for years,
and pastors preach from the pulpits every weekend.
Except for occasional scandalous headlines, much of
the abuse, conflict, and breakdown of pastors, priests,
and rabbis is not in public view. Some of the abuse of
pastors and their families may even look like normal
attrition, or the familiar movement of pastors from one
congregation to another, or a few incompetent pastors

causing conflict. But these appearances mask an insidious trend in organized religion that I call the *clergy killer phenomenon*. That name is an accurate description of both the target and the agenda of this abuse. Clergy killers are terrorists.

This book is a sincere effort to awaken the church to a nightmare coming true. I speak from the experience of many years as a pastoral counselor specializing in the pastoral care, across denominational lines, of clergy and their families. The results of my research and experience, and that of a growing number of concerned leaders, require a responsible cry of alarm and a prophetic warning. We are not just talking about conflict anymore, we are talking about emotional and spiritual abuse of traumatic proportions. And we are discovering that such abuse is exhausting pastors and draining the energy and resources of congregations and denominational programs. This is a prophetic warning, for it warns of an ancient mistake—killing the prophets—that is a forerunner to tribal and national disaster. The record of human history shows that the tribe that kills its shaman loses its soul.

Not only does this book warn of disaster, it provides remedies and effective strategies for healing and health in the church. Church leaders must not allow pastors to die one by one and imagine that this is not a warning signal. And pastors must not allow themselves to slip into victim-thinking, in which they become pitiful shadows of a once noble profession. It will be up to pastors to break this degenerative pattern and move the church forward toward health. Pastors can use a lot of help from concerned laity, seminaries, and wise denominational officials.

Pastors are already networking around this issue. Several organizations, such as the Ministers Mutual Aid, Inc. in Canada and the Association of Battered Clergy in the USA, are working to support and guide pastors who are being abused, as they seek relief and healthy ways to end the abuse.

The first three chapters of this book describe the clergy killer phenomenon in detail. The next four chapters discuss the differences between the common conflicts that occur in any human organization, and the abuse and evil destructiveness now occurring in many congregations. Three types of abusive conflict are described. Then a specific method is offered for managing each one. It is important to note these different categories and methods, for many efforts at negotiation are failing to end the abuse and destruction. Because we must be honest about this abuse process, a chapter is included that describes the *congregation killer*—the pastor who abuses congregations. Though few in number, they too wreak their havoc.

By this time in the book's progression, it will be natural to ask and answer the question of why people act like they do. Chapter 10 discusses a systemic design for human needs and motivations. It is a distillation of the teachings of psychologists and theologians who have attempted to answer this question. The model provided gives an understanding of what pastors must do not only for self-defense, but also to lead congregations toward healing and health.

The themes of Chapters 12 and 13 are the reinvention of clergy support systems and the personal responsibility of pastors for their own spiritual, mental, and physical fitness; pastoral ministry is no longer a safe place for weak or incompetent pastors. These chapters are a strong effort to encourage the growing awareness among clergy that total fitness is required for effective ministry. They also remind us that such fitness need not be an ordeal. It feels great and its benefits are enormous.

Finally, the book concludes with an upbeat description of healthy congregations and an answer to the question, What is health in the spiritual and mental sense, and how can it be achieved? There is great hope that the church will recognize this massive problem and open itself to God's healing, as it has many times before in history. But this will not occur until we can name this demonic reality, exorcise it, and replace it with wholeness. This book is dedicated to that purpose.

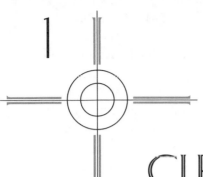

1

CLERGY KILLERS

The first sign of the killing process began at a church board meeting. A member of the board, Tim Johnson said, "A lot of people are complaining to me about Pastor Enright. They're saying he doesn't call enough; he can't be reached when they want to talk to him; and he's not friendly enough."

Board members asked Johnson to identify "a lot of people," but he refused to name them. Then they asked for specific examples. He refused to be specific. The board said they couldn't take action unless they knew the specific complaints. Johnson replied that they had better take action because these were important members who might leave the church.

In response to Johnson's demand, the board set up an investigative team. At the next board meeting, the team reported that they could find no tangible evidence of any problems. Johnson told them the complaints were real and might have something to do with sexual misconduct and misuse of church funds. The investigative team did some more work and again reported, at a later date, no tangible evidence of such misconduct. Johnson then called for a congregational meeting. This request was denied.

Before the next board meeting, a letter filled with innuendoes against the pastor was mailed to the congregation. At the following meeting, the board and Pastor Enright were in a near panic. Johnson said he had talked to the bishop, and the bishop said these were serious charges that needed to be investigated. At a later date, a new investigative team reported that there seemed to be a lot of people unhappy with the pastor. The board voted to have a delegation meet with the pastor.

The pastor was absent from the next meeting. After six months of this harassment, he was in the hospital. The board voted to send a delegation to the bishop and at a following meeting, the delegation reported that the bishop recommended removal of the pastor. By that time, the pastor was scheduled for heart bypass surgery. And it was rumored that his wife had become addicted to tranquilizers.

Pastor Mike Henderson was once a shining star in his denomination. He seemed to have everything going for him. He served a medium-sized, thriving, progressive congregation. Attending there were a couple of university professors and a seminary professor who resented his charisma and success. They combined efforts to sabotage his leadership, though they would not recognize or admit this.

When Henderson's confidence began to falter and his pastoral competence waned under their attacks, they began to accuse him of mental disorders. His wife divorced him in panic. He eventually left ordained ministry and has since been unable to hold any but menial jobs. He now subsists in an inner city, hardly able to cope or even recognize old friends. The clergy killers continue in that congregation, like "scorpions doing what scorpions have to do."

THE NATURE OF THE PROBLEM

These would be sad cases, even if they were unusual. But they are significant because they are not unusual. One informed estimate indicates that a pastor is "fired" (forced out) every six minutes in the United

States. This is a shocking figure, even for those who have been dealing with abuse and conflict in organized religion for many years. Clergy killers are few in number, but awesome in the damage they create. Approximately 60 percent of pastors function competently, even effectively, but at least one-fourth have been forced out of one or more congregations, and many more are severely stressed and vulnerable.

It is also significant that although such incivility reflects the mood of our society, there is little concern at leadership levels for the devastation the clergy killer phenomenon is causing to the mission and spiritual energy of churches and pastors, and to the personal lives of pastors and their families. Seminary curricula and denominational agendas hardly note this critical dynamic. Local congregations and neighborhoods can ignore it, for on the surface things look normal. The church building is still there. The bulletin board on the front lawn announces familiar activities. And the pastor is still in the pulpit on Sundays. Everything looks as it has for years, unless someone notes the stress lines in the pastor's face, and the congregation's lack of enthusiasm for mission programs. Therefore the pastor, and usually spouse and family, suffers quietly and without support.

The name we give this phenomenon is significant. Words such as "disagreement," "clash," or "conflict" do not deliver the wakeup call the church needs. "Clergy killers" tells it like it is, for killing is the agenda, and pastors are the target. My continuing prayer is that the use of this drastic nomenclature will penetrate our illusions that everything is normal, and inspire a search for effective remedies.

Discussing this issue of clergy killers will give courage and clarity to troubled pastors, or at least assure them that they are not alone. Lay people need to be alerted as well; not only do they share responsibility for ending the abuse by clergy killers, they also may become targets. Though the pastor is the typical target for a clergy killer, it is not unusual for the church secretary, organist, moderator, and anyone who openly supports the embattled pastor to also become the object of attack. A random effect, often called "collateral damage," is another form of extended fallout that occurs when clergy killers are unchecked.

Cardiovascular disorders, cancer, arthritis, gastrointestinal disorders, and respiratory problems used to be rare among clergy, and clergy once generated the best mental health and longevity statistics of any profession. Not anymore! Jack McElhaney, President of Ministers Life Resources, Inc. (formerly Ministers Life Insurance Company), recently said that after once being an insurer's dream, clergy now generate statistics and actuarial data similar to the general public.

Wherever I speak to clergy groups these days I encounter pastors who are highly stressed, paranoid, cynical, and even dysfunctional. When I first began to specialize in the pastoral care of pastors and their families in the early 1970s, such characteristics were rare. Now they are common and growing. Many of these maladies are traceable to clergy killers and their effects. The costs to the church are enormous, yet they are somewhat hidden. We have come to believe that high pastoral stress is normal. The church at large is taking a long time to realize that lost clergy, increased health costs for pastors and families, divided congregations, loss of energy for mission, disgust by members who leave, and some malfeasance by pastors can be traced in large measure to the incivility and abuse now common in congregations.

WHO ARE THE CLERGY KILLERS?

Clergy killers are people who intentionally target pastors for serious injury or destruction. We must distinguish them from "normal" persons who disagree with the pastor, injure her or him inadvertently, or even oppose some pastoral project or issue. Later, we will discuss in detail three types of conflict in the church, for these distinctions are important.

Our definition of a clergy killer begins with an understanding of how abnormal a clergy killer is. He or she is not a normal dissident, nor the now typical attitude-challenged parishioner. Generally there are only a few (perhaps only one or two) clergy killers in a given congregation or agency, but they are deadly, and they have expandable influence that typically attracts people with common gripes, frustrations, or misguided agendas. Such often unwitting cohorts can produce a numbing fear in pastor and congregation that hordes of people are organized against them, and that resistance to their agenda will only bring personal injury to the resistors. In reality, however, only the clergy killer is deadly.

Although we must be aware of and discuss clergy killers, we must identify them carefully, because labeling is a dangerous process. Not only can we mislabel someone, we can begin using such pejorative terms to mistreat each other. Therefore, the term "clergy killer" must be used thoughtfully, as well as intentionally. When people see and recognize the clergy killer problem, they must have clear, reliable information so that they may understand and be able to act responsibly.

CHARACTERISTICS

Six "D's" characterize the clergy killer phenomenon:

Destructive: Clergy killers are marked by intentional destructiveness. They don't just disagree or criticize, they insist on inflicting pain and damaging their targets. Their tactics include sabotage, subverting worthy causes, inciting others to do their dirty work, and causing victims to self-destruct.

Determined: Clergy killers don't stop. They may pause, go underground, or change tactics, but they will intimidate, network, and break any rules of decency to accomplish their destruction. They insist that their agenda has priority.

Deceitful: Clergy killers manipulate, camouflage, misrepresent, and accuse others of their own tactics. Their statements and negotiations are not trustworthy.

Demonic: Clergy killers are evil and may be mentally disordered, depending on how you define intentions and behavior that do not yield to patience and love, or honor human decency. Spiritual leaders become symbols and scapegoats for the internal pain and confusion they feel. Because their mental pain and spiritual confusion are unidentified and untreated, they foment unusual, reactive, and destructive motivations. This evil characteristic may also be apparent when there is no other cause that explains the clergy killer behavior.

The mainline church and popular culture essentially have discarded the concept of evil by labeling sin and evil as mental illness or human failure. This loss of a spiritual understanding of intentional destruction leaves us unable to make use of the powerful spiritual gifts of enlightenment, grace, discipline, and courage to confront evil through God's power.

Denial: This fifth "D" indicates the way the church colludes in the agenda of the clergy killer. Most of us don't want to admit to the reality of clergy killers, nor do we acknowledge the intentional damage they cause. Because we believe "this shouldn't be happening in the church," we convince ourselves it isn't really happening. Such denial leaves clergy killers unrestrained and the whole church vulnerable.

Discernment: This is the prescriptive sixth "D." The spiritual gift of discernment is God's grace proffered in an enlightened person who sees and understands evil, and then allows himself or herself to be empowered by God's Holy Spirit and to become an agent of exorcism. Discernment is followed by confronting evil, in this case, the clergy killers. This confrontation works best, of course, in a healthy community of faith.

Another characteristic typical of clergy killers is their intimidating power that they are willing to use to violate the rules of decorum and caring that the rest of us try to follow. This is a powerful weapon at a subconscious level; we sense that such people are willing to escalate the fight and use tactics that we forbid ourselves to use. In fact, most clergy do not even know how to do survival fighting ("street fighting"), much less have the necessary resources and networks for such showdowns.

Clergy killers are masters of disguise *when they choose to be.* They can present themselves as pious, active church members who are "only doing this for the good of the church." Often they convince naive parishioners that they are raising legitimate issues. It is not uncommon for clergy killers to hide among their "allies of opportunity"—members who are their friends or congregational powerbrokers, or members who are disgruntled with the church.

Disguise is irrelevant to many clergy killers, however, for they may find power in fighting openly. They use bluster, threats, and terrorism to appear as unstoppable giants. They intimidate by letting everyone know that they will fight dirty and use any tactic to gain their ends. For most gentle and "peace-at-all-costs" parishioners, such threats are adequate to keep them on the sidelines, allowing the pastor and her supporters to cope the best they can. Such threats are not lost on denominational officials who themselves are usually "nice, churchgoing folks" and who might depend on political support from congregations.

A CLINICAL PERSPECTIVE

A clinical, or psychological perspective on clergy killers indicates that they are likely to have personality disorders (antisocial, borderline, paranoid, narcissistic—which will be discussed later). They may be previous or present victims of abuse. They may have inadequate socialization, arrested adolescence, and violent role models in their history. They may have developed a perverse, voyeuristic, and vindictive taste for the suffering of their victims. In more ordinary terminology, clergy killers have learned the power of throwing tantrums to get their way. They know how to distract, confuse, and seduce. They can wound or kill by direct attacks, by inciting others to inflict the wounds, or by inducing victims to self-destruct.

This self-destruct tactic, in which the victim colludes in his or her victimization, is often subtle, but it is not uncommon. This behavior can be observed among some predators in the animal kingdom. It has also become common in business, politics, and in other professions to harass people in subtle and obvious ways until their distress produces irrational and destructive behavior, or their natural bad habits become toxic. They may wound or destroy themselves or a scapegoat (spouse, boss, friend). They may do something bizarre, unethical, or criminal so that legal authorities must punish them (alcoholism and embezzlement come to mind). Some victims develop behavior and attitudes that lead to alienation of family and friends, divorce, and sometimes loss of credentials. Suicide is a possibility. Understanding how a normal or mentally disordered person becomes a clergy killer is a complicated issue that we will cover in several places later in this book. The identity of a clergy killer is a function of contextual dynamics as well as personal health (physical, mental, and spiritual).

THE CONTEXTUAL DYNAMICS

First, there is *opportunity.* Pastors have become more vulnerable, parishioners more confused and less courageous, denominational offices more political, and our whole society more numb to abuse and conflict. Together these factors create opportunity for abuse of spiritual leaders and even encourage its development.

Another factor is the continued naivete of pastors and the church regarding how mental disorders work. We have become fairly good at noticing, even ministering to obvious mental disorders such as retardation, senility, and so forth. But most people in the church do not understand the pernicious and regressive potential of many mental disorders. Not only do victims of mental disorders become sicker without treatment, their negative influence expands unless they are surrounded by tough love and supervision.

We must be careful not to identify all people in the church who suffer from mental disorders as clergy killers. Most people did not choose their disorder. They need our understanding and ministry in order to return to mental health or competent functioning. But mentally disordered people, especially those with personality disorders, have an above-normal potential to become conflictual, abusive, and clergy killers.

Another dynamic contributing to the formation of clergy killers is the *theological confusion* in organized religion and congregations. One factor in this confusion is our unwillingness to believe in, identify, and do battle with evil. With the development of pop psychology, the church has come to believe that sin and evil can be explained by reference to mental disorders and human failures. With this misguided perspective, we tend to leave mental health and treatment to specialists, and imagine that it therefore has little to do with what goes on in church.

One of the characteristics of evil (this term will be defined later) is its eagerness to exploit human weakness and institutional naivete. Normal people with bad habits and poor self-management skills, mentally disordered people, and spiritually undisciplined people are vulnerable to the power of evil. They may even collude in the influence of evil by choosing evil behavior intentionally, and therefore becoming evil.

Few people consciously choose to become evil, or clergy killers. Evil makes inroads into a system or an individual through a combination of the above dynamics and personal conditions. As evil tendencies and the clergy killer syndrome develop, however, it becomes more likely that a person so afflicted will actually make conscious choices for evil and destruction.

PERSONAL HEALTH

Besides the contextual dynamics that open the door for a clergy killer's deeds, *a person's health*—physical, mental, and spiritual—contributes to the potential for *becoming* a clergy killer. A person who is physically exhausted, ill, or living in a mentally disordered environment is likely to develop mental disorders if such conditions continue for long periods of time. Likewise, a person under great mental stress, indulging in substance abuse, or experiencing biological degeneration for long periods is also vulnerable to mental disorders. A person feeding on spiritual junk food, or who is malnourished spiritually, or who is not conditioned by healthy spiritual disciplines is also more vulnerable than others.

It is the *personality disorders,* however, that seem most likely to lead to the evils a clergy killer perpetrates. The antisocial, borderline, paranoid, and narcissistic personality disorders are readily identifiable by mental health professionals. The *Diagnostical and Statistical Manual of Mental Disorders, Fourth Edition (DSM-IV),* published by the American Psychiatric Association, defines the characteristics of these disorders. Most church members and leaders do not, however, understand how mental illness functions. For our purposes, we will only note that people suffering from mental disorders are often unable to handle leadership responsibilities in the church, and if given them, are likely to abuse them, inadvertently or intentionally.

A GROWING PHENOMENON

Clergy killers are neither figments of imagination nor functions of paranoia. Nearly any experienced pastor or denominational executive has encountered them. I have encountered them or heard of them in every denomination I've worked with. But we tend to deny, excuse, or pamper them in the church. And because we believe love will conquer all (read, "Be nice to everyone"), we pretend to forgive them and love them, while we wish they would also be nice or just go away. Such thinking and behavior do not work.

My research with pastors in Wisconsin and Minnesota (heavily churched states) indicates that 63 percent of pastors know of a colleague who has been seriously abused by a congregation, colleague, or denominational executive. Approximately 25 percent of pastors have suffered such abuse themselves.

In the Winter 1996 issue of *Leadership* magazine, the results of their national survey of Protestant clergy indicated that approximately 23 percent of pastors say they have been fired at least once, and 43 percent said a "faction" (typically less than ten people) forced them out. The reality that so few destructive and evil members can cause so much damage is a grim reminder of Edmund Burke's famous warning, "The only thing required for the triumph of evil is for good men to do nothing." This survey also showed that 41 percent of congregations who fired their pastor have done this to at least two previous pastors. The reasons pastors gave for their terminations included personality conflicts, 43 percent; conflicting visions for the church, 17 percent; financial strain in the congregation, 7 percent; theological differences, 5 percent; moral malfeasance, 5 percent; unrealistic expectations,

4 percent; other, 19 percent. One major denomination reported informally that early in 1996 approximately 2,500 of their pastors had been forced out of congregations already that year.

My experience in conducting seminars on this subject indicates this phenomenon is exploding, as reported by veteran pastors who attend. From sporadic cases in the 1980s to one-quarter to half of present-day pastors, the reports of being abused and forced out appear to be increasing exponentially.

From a more positive perspective, my surveys of Minnesota and Wisconsin clergy indicate that approximately 70 percent feel their lives are normal; 75 percent say there is no major conflict in their parish; 52 percent engage in vigorous exercise and leisure activities; and 83 percent still feel a strong call to pastoral ministry. These are reassuring signs of health in the midst of confusion and pain.

COLLATERAL DAMAGE

Chapter 3 addresses the collateral damage experienced by family members and close associates of the pastor under attack. But the impact of the clergy killer is being felt throughout the church. In fact, one of the causes of the downturn in mainline Protestant denominations is the wounded pastor syndrome. When a pastor is bleeding and desperately trying to survive, she or he will have little energy available for the creative pastoring that church growth requires. But because the pastor is still visible and continues to provide the traditional services, most people do not realize what is occurring. Hardly anyone goes to the pastor with the kind of understanding, strength, and support she or he needs under such circumstances. The pastor in this wounded condition resembles a pet dog with worms. It still looks like a dog, so no one questions the loss of energy and its debilitated functioning.

When I sat at lunch with pastors recently at a conference I was leading on another topic, they talked almost continually of church situations in which the pastor was under attack. Their comments ranged from "There, but for the grace of God, go I" to "Poor guy, I wish I could help him!" This is an indicator of the anxiety and mild paranoia more pastors are feeling as a result of the clergy killer phenomenon.

Several denominational executives have told me recently that as they travel across their district or the nation, they find attacks on clergy to be pandemic. And they often feel helpless to do much about it, because even in strong executive denominations, top leaders have little authority to disarm or fight clergy killers. Denominational leaders fear offending powerful lay leaders, no matter how evil they are. Being politic, they realize that their power is derivative. And most denominational executives do not feel comfortable with the power tactics needed to eliminate clergy killers from a congregation. The current prevalence of lawsuits certainly does not encourage denominational leaders to risk offending hostile-aggressive people (although legal means may be one possibility for controlling clergy killers). This mood in denominational offices is another part of the collateral damage; denominational executives who see and understand clergy killer conflicts often feel guilty about not being able to stop them, even while they spend more time coping with clergy killer problems. Those who deny the clergy killer phenomenon seemingly cannot understand why more denominational resources are being drained by ministries to damaged pastors and congregations.

It would be helpful if seminaries could prepare pastors for the tough realities of the local church. It should be obvious by now that pastors need to learn self-management and survival tactics. And they certainly should be trained in conflict management—the serious kind that clergy killers induce. Moreover, pastors need training in how to help a damaged congregation recover. Lip service to this need is not adequate.

Recently I consulted with an organization that is establishing a leadership training process outside of seminaries. This organization purports to train pastors in evangelism, church growth, and "community-based pastoring." When I asked the director what kind of training they offered pastors in building their own support base, in survival tactics, and in handling collateral damage he looked at me as if I were from another planet. He said, "If a pastor is a dynamic leader, there will be no such problems." His strong bias made it unlikely that he would have listened if I had told him about a burned-out pastor I had talked to the previous week who had graduated from his program, or about at least two other graduates whom I had heard were under attack by clergy killers. The collateral damage is the enormous waste of energy that must be used to help anxious and depressed pastors and congregations do what would be natural if they were healthy, mentally and spiritually. Instead, burdened by clergy killer threat and damage, congregations and pastors flounder and weaken.

Besides the damage to pastor, congregation, denomination, and community, a large part of the clergy killer collateral damage occurs to spouse, family, and other intimates of pastors under attack. As mentioned, this issue will be covered in detail later.

It may be helpful now for you to take some time to write your own thoughts and insights concerning this clergy killer phenomenon. Pages are provided here for you to use.

NOTES

N O T E S

2

CLERGY KILLER
CONTEXT

The etiology or origin of the clergy killer phenomenon is not mysterious, for the church has always
been confronted by evil. But it is important to review
the clergy killer phenomenon in its contemporary context, because this is what is unusual. Unless we consider
its sources, we may not be able to facilitate its cure.

The Bible includes stories of faithful spiritual leaders
under attack. Church history is replete with similar stories. In the 1960s, early warning signals of our present
problems were documented. The cases of one hundred
pastors who had left their congregations under pressure
were analyzed in the little-noticed book, *Preachers in
Purgatory,* by Lester Mondale (Boston: Beacon Press,
1966). Then came studies of pastors by researchers such
as Edgar Mills, John Koval, and Andrew Greeley, who
discovered growing stress among clergy. Several
observers wrote books on this subject, such as *Minister
on the Spot* by James E. Dittes (Boston: Pilgrim Press,
1970) and *Clergy in the Crossfire* by Donald P. Smith
(Philadelphia: The Westminster Press, 1973).

It is the growing presence of incivility and abuse in the
church that has become the greatest source of confusion,

pain, and injustice for pastors. To dislike and criticize a pastor is not uncommon and might even be understandable. But abusing pastors mentally, spiritually, and physically is now a clergy nightmare come true. The growing abuse is also a significant commentary on the mental and spiritual health of the church, for how the church treats its leaders reveals even more about the church than about its leaders. Only a sick or dying church batters its pastors. ("The tribe that kills its shaman loses its soul.")

Contemporary society, moreover, is especially compatible for clergy killers. There is a general distrust of authority figures of any kind. Biblical and theological illiteracy is becoming the norm in the pews. This means parishioners do not understand God's purposes and the dynamics of spiritual leadership, except through their own experience and ideas.

A general sense of entitlement is growing in the church, as well as in society. Church members feel entitled to comfort and privilege. If a pastor does not please them, they feel free to criticize and punish. The business mentality that pervades the church says if the CEO (pastor) does not produce, he should be fired. Related to this is the paradigm shift in ethics and morality. (This "ethic of consequences" will be discussed later.)

Then there are the eager but frustrated parishioners who want to be active in church ministries and leadership, but who find inadequate opportunities for service and then tend to develop a critical attitude. The mobility of parishioners is also part of the context. This means they feel little loyalty to the "peace and unity of the church," since they will soon move on without having to deal with the consequences of their irresponsible behavior.

As has been mentioned, the church today is not training pastors to handle conflict, to support themselves in survival situations, to be disciplined spiritually, nor to be toughminded when their leadership is sabotaged. In this chapter, we will focus attention on several of these conditions to note how they contribute to the clergy killer phenomenon.

SOCIETAL CONTEXT

Entitlement thinking pervades our culture. This is a perversion of the "rugged individualism" that drove early explorers, settlers, and entrepreneurs. As a dynamic middle class emerged through opportunity, hard work, and creativity, many citizens began to think of the earned benefits as rights rather than as the consequences of behavior. Hard work, responsibility, and discipline became optional. Now when entitlement expectations are not met, citizens feel cheated. They assume someone or something other than themselves is to blame. And when they decide who is to blame, they assume the right to punish. Or if the presumed villain is too powerful to be punished, citizens have the right to become vengeful or turn their anger inward and become depressed and dysfunctional. Because the church often reflects society rather than leading it, this entitlement thinking contaminates parish attitudes. It is also a breeding ground for conflict and abuse.

Questioning authority is another characteristic of contemporary society. The questioning is not new; people have long challenged and distrusted leaders. But in the past, those who questioned authority reassured themselves of the leader's legitimacy, or the value of what they were asked to do. Such questioning often helped eliminate poor leaders and facilitate creativity and productivity. Present questioning tends to be more persistent and less responsible. In fact, authority figures easily become targets for contempt and abuse. People's respect for others, which once disciplined our questioning, is waning. Without it, leadership becomes a matter of pleasing the most people. The related loss of internal discipline in groups and organizations suggests that everyone should follow their own instincts, without much attention to shared consequences.

An *ethic of consequences* is another significant factor that contributes to the pervasive incivility. Society has shifted from an ethic based on beliefs to an ethic of consequences. Pragmatists have advocated such a shift for centuries, but the general public insisted that right beliefs must guide behavior. A generation ago Joseph Fletcher shocked the religious world by writing his book, *Situation Ethics* (Philadelphia: The Westminster Press, 1966). He advocated discarding formal beliefs and creeds and managing our lives by the love principle that Jesus taught. This seemed like heresy, not because he advocated love, but because he espoused the questioning of formal belief systems. Now we not only question, but we also ignore or discard formal belief systems.

Contemporary morality clearly reflects two versions of the shift to an ethic of consequences, which is now often called contextualism. According to one version, we should retain traditional beliefs while picking and choosing between them according to convenience of what seems right at the moment. According to the other, we should discard or ignore traditional beliefs and live strictly according to perceived consequences. Without realizing it, however, it is apparent that nearly all of us now make daily decisions based on choosing between what seem like optional sets of consequences, rather than on our religious beliefs.

Living according to anticipated consequences is not new, of course. But establishing this as life's reference point for nearly all citizens is a contemporary phenomenon. Consequences are powerful motivators and a valid test for decision making. Most of us, however, have been socialized to give at least lip service to standard beliefs and are not competent to live without some fixed standards. Moreover, even with computer assistance, we cannot determine all consequences quickly enough to guide our behavior competently.

This is an era of interdependency—shared, cumulative consequences. We are now required to breathe each other's polluted air, drink each other's toxic waste, suffer from each other's irresponsibilities, and pay each other's bills. In society, and now in the church, we are ignoring the rules that guided interdependency for generations. This brings mixed results—some good and some bad. We know we must invent some new and valid guidelines for our behavior. But until that is accomplished, we tend to live by the law of the jungle.

CHANGING CLERGY ROLES

Identity confusion contributes to ineffectiveness when pastors try to lead a changing institution in a changing society. We have already mentioned the loss of authority associated with the clergy role, and the expectation that pastors function as CEOs. But the primary role confusion occurs for pastors when they do what they were trained to do but find this unacceptable to powerful parishioners and unsupported by denominational offices.

In his book *The Purpose of the Church and Its Ministry* (New York: Harper & Row, Publishers, 1956), H. Richard Niebuhr tried to identify the significant shift that was beginning to occur in pastoral leadership during the last generation. He tentatively called the new clergy role "pastoral director." Instead of tending to the traditional spiritual presence and activities, he noted, pastors are expected to spend most of their time directing the congregation's activities and maintaining its facilities.

In another source, Samuel W. Blizzard described how the pastor's role had shifted from what he was trained for (namely, spiritual leadership) to administrative leadership, for which he was not trained ("The Minister's Dilemma," *The Christian Century* 73, No. 17, April 25, 1958). This change produced great stress for pastors. It also forced them to refocus their emphasis and to spend time seeking training in administration.

The pastoral role now includes an unfocused and expanded range of duties. The congregation expects the pastor to be in charge of nearly everything (except activities that the powerbrokers want to control). Being "in charge" here means not only seeing that the activities get done, but also that everyone interested in them is happy with them. From doing the bulletin, to repairing the furnace, to increasing the pledges and enhancing the congregation's image in the community, the pastor must see that everything is taken care of or expect to be blamed when people are disappointed. Because pastors now feel so dependent on the approval of the congregation, it is easier for them to imagine that they are indeed responsible for everything in the congregation. The clinical name for this delusion is codependency, or collusion.

An even stronger version of pastoring in general may be called "megapastoring." This is the expectation on the part of both the congregation and the pastor that the pastor must be, or become, a charismatic personality who can be up front at all church activities, make them successful, and continually draw more new members. The goal, of course, is for the congregation to become a megachurch, with hundreds of enthusiastic members, dozens of thriving programs, and an expanding budget that allows for regular additions to building facilities. As a consequence, the congregation and pastor who do not function like, or look like, a megachurch are suspected of being in decline. The pastor, of course, is blamed and punished.

Changes in roles leave pastors vulnerable in a number of ways. In previous generations a pastor was financially vulnerable, but parishioners and the community usually provided "perks" (half a hog at butchering time, clergy discounts with local merchants, and the like) and general tolerance of ministerial foibles. The pastoral role was respected, and changing pastors required too much effort. Pastors now generally have better salaries, but the traditional supportive perks are gone. Congregational intolerance and the attractiveness of not having to pay a pastor's salary for a while if the congregation fires the pastor, tend to make for frequent moves and unpredictable remuneration for pastors.

A pastor is no longer a power player in many communities. People do not fear the pastor's disapproval, and she is seldom consulted about significant personal, family, and community issues. Along with this change comes an expectation that if a parishioner has serious relational problems, the pastor had better function like a trained mental health professional and resolve the problems. Without the prestige and respect of office, with growing, unrealistic expectations, and with the likelihood of being the scapegoat for parish discontent, the pastor's confidence wanes. Pastors take personally the negative climate in congregations and judicatories today. When people hint that an unhappy, dysfunctional congregation is the pastor's fault, a normal pastoral reaction then is to try harder and to strain for positive change. And yet, because most of the causes of decline and negativity have deep, historic roots, the pastor is unlikely to reverse the trend alone. Moreover, by trying harder to do so, the pastor tends to overreach personal resources and to neglect physical, mental, and spiritual disciplines that would promote health. This makes the pastor even more vulnerable.

In recent years a new arena of vulnerability has been introduced—the legal system. Until the infamous Nally Case in California in 1979, it was nearly unthinkable for pastors to be sued in secular courts. (In this case, the parents of a young man who committed suicide while in the pastor's care sued the congregation and pastor for negligence.) The regulation of church facilities and activities by state legislatures was not an issue. Today, suing and regulating pastors are not only possible but regular occurrences. Since state and local regulations apply to churches and because pastors have been sued successfully, many pastoral activities must be considered from a legal perspective. A career can be lost and financial resources drained when secular law enters the church. But it is the fear of such possibilities that does the most damage. Pastors now worry about legal issues, second-guess their own behavior, or simply avoid some legitimate but legally sensitive ministries.

Pastors are not blameless. About 10 percent of pastors have engaged in sexual malfeasance. (See my book *Ministry and Sexuality: Cases, Counseling and Care* [Minneapolis: Augsburg Fortress, 1990].) My research also indicates that up to 15 percent of pastors are extremely susceptible to such temptations and that other forms of moral misconduct are potentially present in their lives. Such malfeasance warrants legal review and recourse. It should not, however, blind us to the inappropriateness of many legal incursions into church and pastoral practices, or to the reality that the vast majority of pastors are competent and reliable.

Another area of vulnerability lies in various forms of discrimination against clergy. Clergy have experienced racism and sexism. But more recently, clergy are vulnerable to ageism. Though good church folk do not admit it because this is a legally sensitive matter, pastors over age fifty can expect to be criticized and encouraged to leave congregations where parishioners want younger leaders. The call process is notorious for bypassing older pastors or relegating them to less attractive parishes.

The deterioration in clergy mental health statistics was mentioned earlier. This growth in breakdowns reflects what is occurring in society as a whole, of course. Here are some approximate, yet reliable data gleaned from my counseling with pastors since 1970. The numbers in each category have grown from near zero to the figures listed.

- ➤ Burnout (exhaustion to the point of malfunction)
    clergy: 15 percent
    general population: 8–12 percent

- ➤ Divorce (once or more)
    clergy: 15 percent (some denominations much higher than this)
    general population: 30–40 percent

- ➤ Chemically dependent (professional impairment through use of alcohol and other substances)
    clergy: 5 percent
    general population: 10–12 percent

- ➤ Mental disorder (inability to function normally)
    clergy: 2 percent
    general population: 8–10 percent

- ➤ Moral malfeasance (immorality)
    clergy: 10 percent
    other helping professions: 12–15 percent

These and other indicators of the vulnerability of pastors make it apparent that the traditional support systems for clergy are no longer adequate.

INSTITUTIONAL CONTEXT

We still call ourselves by familiar denominational names, but the traditional beliefs and practices that characterized them are eroding rapidly. *Loss of traditional identity* marks the consciousness and behavior of institutionalized religion in this generation. Without such informed identity to guide our life in the community of faith, we must invent new identities by consensus.

Given the easy mobility of church members, the cultural and ethnic diversity, and the ethic of consequences, people feel less loyalty to a single tradition. While trying to be accepting, adaptive, and caring toward the more diverse community, we have not yet found many common beliefs and practices that inspire loyalty. Parishioners no longer see diversity as important.

Some talk of "reinventing the church." This sounds like a good idea in some ways, for clearly revisions are needed. But when tradition is challenged, believers become confused. The result of changes tends to leave us angry and cynical; human beings do not handle change well when there are no reliable guidelines or leaders. The pastor is likely to become a lightning rod for such feelings.

The simplest version of our democracy is "one person, one vote." This becomes the model in the church when traditional beliefs and polities are abandoned. In appearance the church still has leaders, institutions, and traditional beliefs and practices. But the individualistic perspective of parishioners leaves pastors without authority, elected leaders with little responsibility, and the community of faith with little accountability for individual behavior.

The *business model* is operative in organized religion. Congregations and denominations are run as if they were businesses. This means that the pastor is expected to function as a CEO, the parishioners get to act like stockholders and customers, and finances are the "bottom line."

The business model is fine in itself, but the church was not called to be a business. And when it operates as one, it tends to lose its mission. Moreover, when pastors, who were not trained to be CEOs, are evaluated by that model, they become confused and ineffective, and feel highly stressed because they are trying to be something they are not. This leaves the stockholders/customers unhappy. With entitlement thinking rampant, members feel free to criticize and even punish the pastor for their unhappiness.

Meanwhile, the sense of mission that unites a healthy community of faith is lost in the concern over budgets and powerbrokers. Conflict is inevitable.

Triage is a medical term designating the decision-making process used when there are inadequate resources to meet urgent needs. Physicians and nurses traditionally made the triage decisions in health care situations, until the concept of "managed care" emerged. Many mainline denominations and congregations today use triage to address conflict.

In institutional religion, we always hope and pray that the necessary triage would be guided by a consensual sense of mission, and by pastors and respected lay leaders. It is apparent, however, that much of the call for triage in the church is produced by near panic as membership and resources decline continually. Traditional leaders become obsessed by making political decisions regarding resources and programs. Congregants are focused on budgets. And clergy, who are not prepared for any of this, become the scapegoats for the general unhappiness triage produces.

We can do better than this. When spiritual leaders understand that triage can be a necessary and healthful process, it can be managed with spiritual discipline and sensitivity. Typically, the church tends to conduct triage through politics (favored persons, programs, and methods). This is not all bad, as we know; yet three factors can cloud our perception of what is needed. The first of these, as already mentioned, is the near panic in denominational offices and congregations when income no longer matches policies and programs. When panic guides decision making, fear and the law of the jungle are dominant, no matter how dedicated the decision makers try to appear.

The second beclouding factor is that "downsizing" and becoming "lean and mean" are dominant themes in society. This attitude has several roots, but the one that drives much of this triage is what Stephen Covey calls the "Scarcity Mindset" in *The Seven Habits of Highly Effective People* (New York: Simon & Schuster, 1989). This mindset is an outgrowth of the illusion, beyond the reality of shortages, that major resources are in short and declining supply—therefore, smart people had better grab what they can and cut expenses to the bone. According to Covey's perspective, "the Scarcity Mentality is the zero-sum paradigm of life." People with this attitude have trouble sharing, accepting change, planning positively, and believing the best about other people. Covey contrasts this attitude with the "Abundance Mentality," which celebrates life, individual worth and uniqueness, the goodness in human beings, and the likelihood that there will be enough for everyone if resources are managed wisely. This mentality does not encourage irresponsible consumerism. Rather, it is a positive perspective that encourages wise management.

We would think that the church would be a leader in propounding abundance mentality. Instead, the contemporary church is marked by its acceptance of a scarcity mentality. By implication and behavior, it teaches that there is a shortage of everything from salvation (we alone have it), to money (people can only be expected to give so much), to inspiring vision (let's not be unrealistic). When scarcity is already the mindset and the church faces an obvious need to recognize loss of members and income, the ensuing triage will be political and regressive.

Pastors get caught in this version of triage, for it is modeled at the highest levels and demanded at the local congregational level. Even optimistic, dedicated pastors are often unable to stem the tide of triage based on scarcity, so they succumb to and may even be victimized by it. When a congregation lives by the bottom line, and shortages appear, it is likely the pastor who is blamed and whose salary and support services are cut. When the scarcity mindset prevails, there is also little vision of a higher possibility, the third clouding factor. And if the pastor proposes one, he is likely to be called unrealistic at best. Moreover, he is still expected to produce reassuring sermons, exciting programs, and manage the church budget without causing discomfort to anyone but himself. It is not difficult to see that triage is fertile ground for clergy killers.

An *empowered but untrained laity* is a contextual factor that usually invites problems. This has become an unexpected consequence of the seemingly noble concept that church leadership should be shared between laity and clergy. Clergy are trained for their share of leadership. Lay persons usually are not. When power is equal but training and perception are not, conflict is inevitable. In the hope of avoiding this conflict, the church has generated an enormous number of training courses. Several relevant factors were missed, however.

One is that the people who need training most often do not receive it. Another is that training materials often do not incorporate insights from the psychological disciplines about such issues as denial, projection, defensiveness, ego struggles, and competition—insights that would help lay leaders understand how the group functions (see chapter 10) and how best to guide that group. Laity may gain knowledge in the typical leadership training materials, but they seldom learn to change their natural habits and style, nor do they learn to be accountable for what their leadership produces. The inevitable cost factor and the typical congregational inertia often makes even the best training materials irrelevant.

Training materials for lay leaders seldom include study and implementation of denominational polity and local congregation bylaws. Yet these are some of the most valuable resources for managing conflict and clergy killer abuses. We often now "empower" the laity, but without training, spiritual discipline, and accountability they are likely to become ineffective leaders, "loose cannons," even attitude-challenged malcontents.

At the root of these institutional context factors that encourage the development of clergy killers, is the *deterioration of spiritual health*. When people are malnourished and sick physically, they will tend not to behave in healthy ways. When they are mentally ill, they will tend to think irrationally. And when they are spiritually unhealthy, they will ignore spiritual disciplines and seek panaceas in spiritual junk food. Because spiritual health will be discussed more fully later on, it is simply noted here as a primary factor in the growing prevalence of clergy killers.

You may find it useful now to add your own ideas about the clergy killer context on the pages provided here.

NOTES

N O T E S

3

COLLATERAL DAMAGE

Note: This chapter is written especially for people related to an abused pastor—spouse, family, close friends ("intimates," as they will be called here).

"Collateral damage" is a military term that designates the damage done to areas and people near to a military target that has been hit with explosive weapons. It also illuminates a painful phenomenon in organized religion. Spouses, family members, and close associates of a deeply distressed or abused pastor often suffer such collateral damage. It is not uncommon for them to be irreparably damaged, because they typically do not have even the minimal support and protection afforded to pastors who are stressed or under attack. The following case study illustrates this.

CASE STUDY: "ABUSE OF CLERGY SPOUSE AND CHILDREN"

It was 2:00 in the morning, and she was still wide awake. Her wakefulness was unusual, for she usually had no trouble sleeping. In her mind she kept reviewing the heated comments made earlier that evening by several parishioners at a specially called congregational meeting.

They initially had been condemning her husband with vicious and untrue accusations she had heard before. But now they were attacking her, saying she gossiped about them, refused to help around the church, and was driving away beloved old members of the congregation. She couldn't believe her ears! Then she heard parishioners accusing her daughter of being immoral and her son of being a "pervert." While these attacks were going on, some parishioners were actually applauding.

Inside her, it felt like a fuse blew and the lights went out. She was numb. And then the rage overwhelmed her. She felt herself jumping to her feet, shouting "No! No! No!" It was as if it were another woman who ran down the aisle, grabbed her children away from friends they were sitting with, and rushed out of the church with them. She barely remembered driving them home.

Now she was alone in bed. She knew her husband was sitting downstairs in his study. The children were in their rooms, but she didn't know what they were doing or thinking. Alternately she sobbed and raged. "What in the world is happening?" she asked, alone in the darkness.

Over a year ago, a former social worker (a single woman who had been fired from her job) and the wife of a church board member had brought some strong complaints about the pastor to the board. For several meetings, board members listened to their complaints but did nothing about them. Then at the annual congregational meeting, ten members got up unexpectedly and said they were withdrawing their pledges until the pastor resigned.

The board immediately agreed to set up an investigative team. Now, several months later, a congregational meeting had been called to vote on their report. After the pastor's wife had fled the meeting, several members arose to defend the pastor and plead for decency. But a congregational vote was taken, and a majority voted to fire the pastor.

She looked over at the clock. It was 6:00 a.m., time to get ready for work and help the kids get ready for school. "What are we going to do now?" she kept asking herself.

This painful case is not as unusual as it sounds. When intimates of abused pastors gather, they tell stories like this and often weep together. In some places they are beginning to find each other, to care for each other, and to plan remedial action. If you are a traumatized spouse, family member, or dear friend of a battered clergy person, this chapter will probably make more sense to you than to those who cannot believe such things happen in the church. What you might not realize is that you must act on your own behalf to heal from such attacks and to recover a peaceful, satisfying life.

PASTORAL ROLE

Why should any of this concern the church and synagogue? After all, stress and abuse are now occurring in other vocations as well. Criticism and conflict "go with the territory" in professional ministry. Shouldn't pastors be strong enough to handle these pressures and protect their families from collateral damage?

In order to understand the painful phenomenon of collateral vulnerability and collateral damage among intimates of the pastor, we need to review some pertinent realities about the contemporary role of pastor.

1. The pastoral role is engulfing. This is the only professional role in which a person's professional practice, personal identity, and religious faith are all wrapped up in a single package. In other words, there is no escaping, except through anonymity. Even then, the pastor herself seldom forgets her role and others' expectations of it. People in other vocations can at least escape into their religious faith when the pressure is on.

2. When a person marries a pastor or is intimately related to a pastor, the person is normally expected to take some interest in and to participate at some level in this role. The participation can vary from simply listening to the pastor talk about his experiences to becoming the unpaid "assistant pastor." Even if a pastor's intimates can separate themselves from his role, the congregation and perhaps the denomination still will have at least some role-related expectations of them.

3. The clergy spouse and other intimates often do not have a safe person or place to turn to when they need to sort out the distress of collateral damage and find dependable support. They may have some kind of personal support system of their own to help manage this distress. But typically such people feel anxiety for the pastor, besides their own pain. Mixed feelings of

helplessness and impulses to fight back blend with anger that "this" is happening and the church is letting "it" happen.

4. Intimates of a distressed or abused pastor are likely to have unwanted and intense feelings about what is happening. Such feelings are normal for human beings under unusual stress, but may be surprising when they occur. The intimates experience added stress when these normal reactions are misunderstood, condemned, or ignored by the church. It should be no surprise that the personal faith, loyalty to the church, and even the health and marriages of such people are threatened or seriously damaged under such circumstances. Further, it should not surprise us that some become assertive or hostile-aggressive in their reactions toward those they blame, toward themselves, and toward the pastor.

5. A growing number of clergy intimates, however, are taking steps to protect and care for themselves. Some clergy intimates:

- Develop a stronger faith that is not dependent upon their congregation or denomination.
- Develop a personal support system independent of the church, but that may include other clergy intimates.
- Align themselves more supportively with the pastor to whom they relate.
- Develop closer family relationships so that the whole family can survive the distress and heal and grow together as a result.
- Organize support groups of battered spouses and intimates who not only survive together, but who also support, challenge, and grow synergistically.
- Write books and articles to let the church and society know that such acute distress and abuse occur, and what to do about it. Artistically inclined intimates are using a variety of art forms, not only for survival, but to share the import of their experience with others.

LEARNED PATTERNS

Intimates are experiencing collateral damage side by side with pastors who themselves are being abused, burning out, suffering the negative consequences of their own malfeasance, or are in traumatic transitions. We should note in review how clergy tend to respond to their stress because what affects one person in a close relationship affects the intimates. It can be helpful for intimates of a pastor to understand the patterns of thinking and behavior that develop as deep distress occurs.

Systems theory reminds us that not only do close partners affect each other, but also that the system in which they participate has a life of its own. The health of the system in which they participate, as well as their own health, becomes a matter of interdependence. Further, every system is part of other systems. Therefore, depending on the level of dependencies, participants and systems generate shared and cumulative consequences.

Clergy, just like all people who suffer from deep distress, tend to manage their pain according to learned patterns and personality types. These response patterns are built upon the more primary agendas of human behavior discussed in Chapter 10.

EXPECTATIONS

Each person has a mental image of his or her strengths and weaknesses, dreams and expectations about the vocational and relational choices he or she makes. The degree to which these expectations are met strongly influences self-esteem. In recent times, a sense of entitlement ("I have a right to _____") has become part of individual and group expectations. These become intense and confused under pressure.

SENSE OF MEANING

By the time people are adults, they have developed a sense about what life means, although not all people are aware of or can articulate their own sense of life's meaning. That meaning, however, shapes an understanding of what is morally right or wrong. This dimension is even stronger than a person's expectations, although the two are related, for they allow people to judge behavior on what seems to be a universal scale. A person's perspective on life's meaning informs them about good and evil and about their relationship to God. For example, when I assume that God is part of what is happening to me, the implications are awesome. Finally, when I apply my senses of morality and spirituality to the universe, I adopt a life view that provides the stage setting (context) for experience through history and into the future.

PAIN THRESHOLD

An imaginary line in the psyche separates stimuli into conscious and unconscious, tolerable and intolerable experience. The line has to do with comfort levels of body, mind, and spirit. When stimuli stay below the line, they are tolerable and subconscious. When they rise above the line, they become conscious, painful, and intolerable—and we react. Pain reduction and coping behavior are instituted. It is apparent that pain thresholds and coping behaviors vary individually.

MINDSET

This is the mental reservoir of beliefs, habits, and experiences from which a person chooses a way of thinking about what is happening to him or her personally. At a subconscious level, the mind picks and chooses from the above dynamics to compose a personhood and base for reaction to experiences. Mindset is what shows in body language, facial expressions, and behavior patterns. It tends to be reactive, that is, it can be influenced rather quickly by circumstances that seem to have deep meanings. Mindset is important to decision making, for it will determine immediate behavior unless a more rational process is established.

STRATEGIES

When a clergy intimate experiences collateral damage due to a close relationship with the pastor, or because he or she is being attacked personally, strategies for managing the damage have specific characteristics. First, intimates are not usually ordained and therefore have limited access to denominational and congregational communication channels and resources. Consequently, coping strategies are put in place apart from these channels and resources. Second, clergy intimates do not have the aura of the clergy role to provide means of control and support as elements of the strategy. Third, there is a flavor of unfairness attached to collateral pain, for a clergy intimate often does not feel deserving of such treatment. Therefore, coping strategies often involve a search for vindication. Finally, clergy intimates live with expectations and limitations they may not have understood or chosen.

Clergy spouses tend to feel deep impact from collateral damage, thus their reactions and proactions tend to be strong. The impact of the damage may be lessened if the spouse has interests outside the church (vocation, activities, support). Where emotional impact is deep, spouses of both genders react with socialized tendencies—dependence, competition, possessiveness, and so forth. If the distress becomes profound, the desperate "fight-flight" syndrome is triggered. At this survival level, a rational perspective is difficult to sustain. Consequently, it is important to understand these normal response patterns before they happen, if possible. Or, if they are already happening, to at least know what they are all about.

Whether the pastor is married or single, and whether or not the family includes children, there is an obvious need to keep relationships with intimates functioning in a healthy manner. Therapy may be needed when stress is severe and sustained. Generally, the distress should not be kept secret from children and intimates, except for confidential matters. Children should be helped to talk about the difficulties, given information appropriate to their questions and needs, and provided adequate comfort and positive diversion along with normal routines.

Networking is a common response for clergy spouses. Here a spouse initiates or responds to interactions with people who are supportive, or people who have had similar experiences. The network may include old or new relationships, and wise or unwise attachments. If the networking is reactive (based on emotions and habits), then the network will be used and perhaps manipulated to meet felt needs and support present perceptions. If the networking is proactive (rational and creative), then the spouse will be helped to assess situations, be held accountable for behavior, and receive guidance about ways to respond, as well as receive comfort and support.

Action groups can be formed to expand the impact of responses to collateral damage. These may have both reactive and proactive dimensions, but they typically include an organizing-planning dimension and provide a synergy that empowers strategy. The strategy of action groups may focus on redress, an attempt to correct, heal, and gain restitution for the pain. It may focus on seeking long-term changes in various systems in order to benefit present survivors and protect potential victims. And it may focus on a combination of goals, including the distractions and joys of working and being together.

"Lonerism" is always a possibility for people experiencing collateral damage. This is a negative strategy in which clergy intimates separate themselves from positive resources and wallow in misery (sometimes called "victim thinking"). Such a reaction is normal at first, as the person retreats figuratively into the fetal position. But the strategy is often ineffective in stopping the abuse or pain, and it is deadly to long-term health. A healthy person

tends to move to a survivor mode in which the pain and damage are acknowledged and normal reactions are accepted, but these are turned toward healthy, creative, and proactive strategies.

Group responses occur also, for it is not only clergy and their intimates who are pained and damaged when pastors are stressed and abused. The ripple effect spreads the damage. Some damage is obvious, some is subtle. Some damage is immediate, some is long term. Some damage causes destruction, some causes pain that is transformed into growth and mission. How this pain and damage affects groups and organizations is a function both of normal reactions and more rational proactions, because groups and organizations have feelings and responses like the individuals who are part of them.

Congregations whose pastor and intimates undergo deep distress and damage usually will not produce homogeneous reactions and responses. Members who do the damage, and those who abet them, may experience guilt, dismay, and denial if they are sensitive to the damage. If such members are blamed, they may point at others, assert that the pastor was at fault and deserved punishment, and even express self-righteousness about their behavior. Members who support the pastor and try to defend her will likely experience such emotions as guilt, denial, and fear; they may feel they should have been more protective, wonder whether they did all they could, or fear the attackers may come after them. Bystanders tend to feel shock, denial, and confusion because they can't imagine how this could occur, or they believe it shouldn't have and therefore will go away easily. Some can't figure out what is going on.

Denial is a big part of this phenomenon, for most people think this shouldn't happen in the church. Therefore, they minimize it, treat it as an aberration, or deny its existence. Such denial limits the possibility that people will do anything constructive about the abuse. Congregations have major responsibility for the treatment of their pastors. They are the reason the pastor is there. They expect the pastor to care for them. They take vows to care for the pastor in return, as part of a healthy ministry relationship. When it is members of the faith community who are doing the damage, this affects the congregation's mission negatively, in addition to the damage done to pastor and intimates, and the identity of the congregation is called into question.

Congregations are often unhealthy spiritually and clinically. They are loosely organized, except for the powerbrokers who have an organized following. They do not know and understand their denomination's polity. They have all they can do to manage their own problems and the hangover of old problems in the congregation. Furthermore, they do not understand that the health of the pastor is crucial to the health of the congregation. Thank God, there are also many healthy congregations. These are unlikely to abuse their pastors, at least for very long. There are even some congregations fortunate enough to have avoided such problems . . . so far.

Denominational officials tend to have mixed reactions to the high levels of distress among clergy and the abuse many are suffering. These officials have even greater ambivalence about collateral damage. They feel very real concern for hurting, abused pastors and their intimates, but they make little effort to correct the basic issues behind these symptoms. When officials face this abuse phenomenon honestly, it seems beyond control. Other officials express doubt that there is a serious problem. Some believe pastors bring their suffering on themselves through incompetence and poor management habits. And some simply say they don't know what the correct response should be and don't have the time or finances to find out. It is also apparent that it has become standard practice for denominations to "fire the coach when the team is losing," or at least not go to bat for a suffering pastor. Most of these reactions are the result of a predictable, self-protective state of denial.

At the same time, we must take into account the realities of a typical denominational office. Top-level officials derive their offices through a political process. Politics in the church tends to be a mixture of pleasing powerful persons and groups while honoring the theology and traditions of the denomination. Those who benefit from such a process tend to see the theology and tradition as good. Those who do not perceive themselves as benefiting tend to see it from a negative perspective. Along with the politics, good and bad, the denomination's polity guides and limits denominational responses to pastoral distress.

A third reality is the triage occurring in nearly all denominational offices. Triage is, as discussed earlier, a medical term referring to the life-and-death decisions medical professionals must make in emergency situations when needs are greater than resources. With long-term membership and financial losses, most denominations now feel similar emergency conditions and have begun to practice triage by deciding which people and programs will receive the dwindling dollars. Therefore newer programs, such as support for distressed clergy and their families, are unlikely to be funded adequately. For a long time the church at large has assumed that pastors could, or should, be able to take care of themselves. But the clergy role and its challenges have changed, while clergy training and support have not. Some denominational officials, however, are seeing that the health of clergy is crucial to the health of the church. It is unlikely that abusive congregations will become healthy until the care and support of spiritual leaders again becomes top priority.

A PERSONAL STRATEGY

There are no miraculous, quick fixes for either clergy or their intimates who suffer collateral damage. While we pray and do everything we can to remedy the deep distresses of spiritual leaders, it is apparent that each leader and each intimate of such leaders must accept responsibility for his or her own protection, healing, and growth. Because each person has unique characteristics, no one remedy will fit all. But we can indicate factors shown to promote the well-being of clergy and intimates. Then each person must pick and choose from available strategies to build a recovery and support system in concert with those who care and others who suffer.

1. **Awareness.** This is the starting place for dealing with nearly any problem or opportunity. We must see the situation as clearly as possible, examine it carefully, then be honest with ourselves about causes and remedies. This awareness is achieved through our own honest appraisal, a search for fresh information and perspective, and an openness to God's gift of discernment. We often need a competent partner to develop this awareness.

2. **Self-assessment.** This is a deliberate appraisal of personal strengths, weaknesses, resources, habits, and helpful methods for dealing with deep distress. Again, most of us need a competent partner for this work.

3. **Personal support system.** Evaluate your system. Is it adequate? How do you need to improve it? Is the give-and-take between you and the support system realistic? Support systems are described in more detail in Chapter 12.

4. **A plan.** Develop a strategy for positively managing this deep distress. Because most of us do not develop a clear strategy for managing abuse before it occurs, we must then devise such a strategy under pressure. The

strategy for managing wounds, however, can be helpful for managing abuse: stop the bleeding; check for and treat other damage; go to a safe place for healing and recovery; then get on with your life, without letting this injury determine your whole perspective.

5. **A dream.** Develop a healthy life perspective and strategy that allows you to complete recovery, prevent recurrence, and provide a satisfying positive mission for your life.

6. **A community.** Blend this self-care strategy with that of those close to you.

7. **A positive attitude.** How and when you get out of this distress will depend upon whether or not you deny the distress; what kind of strategy you develop for managing it; how healthy you are physically, mentally, and spiritually; how helpful your support system is; and what kind of attitude you have. Your attitude (what you tell yourself about the pain you are feeling) becomes a crucial ingredient in your recovery. Here are some typical "attitudes": "It's not my problem." "God will take care of this." "With some help from God and my support system, I can handle this." "I can turn this into a learning, growing experience, with God's guidance and the comfort from my support system."

If you select one of the first two attitudes or something like them, you have a difficult road ahead. If the pastor is suffering and you relate to him, you must deal with some negative consequences, whether you want to or not. To say "it's not my problem" is a statement of denial. Denial may seem to help, but it forces the realities of your collateral damage into your unconscious mind. It is difficult to deal with problems wisely in this condition. And if you believe that God will take away all your pain, you are missing the point of many Bible stories.

People who look outside themselves for help and support have a very good prognosis, for these are the kinds of attitudes that lead to good self-management, recovery, and growth, according to my research on pastors and their families. When you have recovered from collateral damage, you may find it worthwhile to watch for other victims of collateral damage. You may be a godsend to that person through your listening, experience, and prayers.

In summary, if you are close to a pastor who is deeply distressed about being attacked and abused, it is likely that you will share the pain to some extent. You may even become the target of abuse yourself. How deeply you suffer depends on many things: how well or how poorly the pastor handles this distress, how much of the pain you are willing to share, how much of the attack is directed toward you, what tolerance you have developed for mental and spiritual pain, and what strategy you select for managing your trauma. Collateral damage need not become a terminal condition, but it might. With wise management and support, victims can become survivors and get on with their lives and mission.

You might find it helpful, if you haven't already done so, to take some time now to write your own story of collateral damage. Pages are provided for this purpose.

N O T E S

IS CONFLICT
IN THE CHURCH
NORMAL?

Yes, conflict in the church is normal. But incivility and abuse are not.

If we want healthy congregations and pastors, conflict is healthy because it helps keep communication open and honest. It promotes authenticity by recognizing diversity; it teaches us how to be a community of faith rather than an artificially homogeneous group. And it helps us to keep learning and being creative.

Like any expression of energy, however, conflict can become dangerous and destructive for everyone. Therefore, we must continue to learn how to manage well our expressions of energy—emotions, ideas, explorations, interactions, and ministry.

Pendulum swings are common in human interactions. Today the pendulum of church manners has swung far to the negative side. There is a significant amount of incivility, fighting, and abuse in congregations and denominations. This conflict is having a deleterious effect on the character and mission of the church in general. Moreover, we tend to react to the conflict by arguing about who is to blame, whether there is more conflict than before, and what clever programs will make the conflicts go away.

The reality is that conflict is present and can be both useful and debilitating. The following generalizations can be made about our current conflict and ways of coping with it:

»• Conflict is real, persistent, and sometimes mean.

»• Conflict can be normal, abnormal, or spiritual.

»• Conflict can escalate into abuse and inflict collateral damage.

»• Conflict can be managed poorly or well.

»• Effective conflict management is not yet the norm in congregations or judicatories.

THE CONTEXT

Understanding the context in which events occur is crucial to understanding the events themselves, for the events do not occur in vacuums. Further, the context often provides early warning signals of significant change, as do storm clouds on the horizon. The context gives major clues about how resolution may be achieved, like when we look for shelter from the storm. Context also provides a foundation for realistic evaluation of both the conflict and attempts at resolution, as when we note how big the storm clouds are and what the weather forecast says.

Our image of the ideal church doesn't include conflict. This is unrealistic, of course, but this fallacy about the church is a significant part of the context; when we imagine that conflict shouldn't exist, we are likely to engage in denial when conflict does arise. And as all pop psychology enthusiasts know, when we are in denial, we have difficulty seeing and believing what we deny, we are likely to misinterpret or excuse it, and we are unable to use our best rational resources to resolve or manage it. But conflict among church members has now become so obvious, persistent, and painful that we can no longer deny or minimize it.

Dissension, vindictiveness, and abuse have always existed in organized religion, but not to the extent that we see them today. Although denominations have endured internal strife, bitter feuds, and splits in the past, it is frightening, as well as embarrassing, to see how many religious leaders are willing to destroy careers, congregations, and missions in the name of theological cleansing, or whatever the source of their vexation.

While an outside observer has little difficulty seeing the selfishness, ambition, hypocrisy, and sinfulness in these struggles, the people involved always manage to rationalize and justify their actions. Resorting to secular legal remedies is an indicator of the factiousness of our struggles.

Besides the idealization of the church and a blindness to reality, there are other causes and contributors to contemporary church conflict. You might find it useful to review Chapter 2 which discusses the context of the clergy killer phenomenon. Besides those contextual issues, several other factors are specifically related to conflict itself.

THEOLOGICAL CLEANSING

Theological movements have come and gone throughout the church's history, and the intensity of the conflicts surrounding them has increased and decreased. Today many truculent church members believe we should seek conformity, even homogeneity, in belief and practice. Such crusaders demand that all participants adhere, at least verbally, to some doctrinal statement or creed. They reserve to themselves the right to condemn, ostracize, or expel nonconformists.

The mild version of theological cleansing advocates what we have come to call "political correctness." In this mindset, certain terms and rituals ("*shibboleths*," Judges 12:6) are deemed to be prime indicators of acceptability by those intent on cleansing. Violations consist of incorrect terminology, rituals that offend heightened sensitivities, and policies that do not incorporate selected causes. Theological cleansing is typically enforced through putdowns, shaming, harassment, and even public censure of nonconformists. A cleansing crusade may be an attractive vehicle for clergy killers, for it seems useful to the more vicious personality types. However, it can be used as a first stage in the movement toward more serious conflict and abuse. Therefore, it must be noticed and managed by responsible leaders, lest it escalate.

We must note the difference, however, between cleansing crusades and legitimate correcting and disciplining of believers who are in serious theological or polity error (refer to 2 Timothy 2:14–16 and 3:16, 17). This is not an easy distinction to make in times of conflict, for each side views itself as being correct. A significant indicator, however, is vindictiveness. Those who are unwilling to negotiate disagreements and who demand punishment are usually on a cleansing crusade. (Chapter 15 of Acts is a primary guide to healthy management of conflict.)

INFRASTRUCTURE COLLAPSE

Several factors have tended to mitigate and control church conflict in the past. The extended family, socialization, and healthy leadership have helped "keep the lid on" in previous generations.

Many people are noting the disintegration of a healthy extended family structure. The church feels the effects because the extended families in a congregation were usually "good folks" who knew and supported each other intimately and loyally. Though they usually had their weaknesses, such family systems did not ordinarily promote incivility and abuse. Members of such families naturally migrated to positions of leadership and thereby extended caring and support, at least to members who were family-approved. If conflict developed, it would be handled in the usual extended family process. Family members would talk over the issues among themselves and come to a consensus, which then influenced the congregation toward this consensus. Conflicts among extended families were handled in whatever time-honored method had worked in previous generations.

It is obvious that some extended families were ruled by tyrannical patriarchs or matriarchs, but this was not the norm. Some extended families hid their abuse and secrets, which tended to produce tragically flawed citizens. We must not idealize the extended family, but neither should we ignore the values and support it produced for many citizens. The nuclear family model and the single-parent family models are demonstrating serious flaws as well. So we are looking for the healthiest characteristics of all family system models in search for healthy interaction among church members.

ELDERSHIP

We live as a culture of adolescents—irresponsible and intentionally immature. We no longer value the wisdom of age and experience. In fact, ageism is causing us to disregard the wisdom of experience, to be insensitive to the aging process, and to warehouse and abuse our elders. When youthfulness is worshiped, the socialization, support, and insight traditionally provided by elders is lost. Aging people, who could be productive and stabilizing, are often regarded as "out of it" and a burden to be endured until they die. What a loss!

Elders can tyrannize, of course. And if they continue to be abused as they increase in number and proportion, we can expect ageism to produce reactions similar to the rage and violence induced by racism and sexism.

What we need instead, and are in danger of losing, is the patient, sensitive, thoughtful "cool" that wise elders can provide.

VOLCANO EFFECT

A "melting pot" society is like a boiling cauldron. Congregations are like this. When the unique pressures of church life (triage resulting from declining membership and budgets, less spiritual discipline, frustration when the church or pastor do not provide comfort, and so forth) are added together, we get a boiling effect that rises to volcanic dimensions. A shock factor is added, which tends to produce confusion; people do not expect the church to function this way. Parishioners traditionally expect peace, reassurance, guidance, and hope from the church. Instead there exists much chaos.

ANGER

This powerful term fits the normal reaction to all these upsetting dynamics in society and the church. Anger is closely related to the volcano effect just described.

We know that anger is a normal response to violated expectations. We also know that the anger response is automatic. Human beings, much like animals, have learned habits that determine what will trigger their anger. We do have a choice about how we will manage this strong emotion. When healthy anger management models and habits are not present, however, anger is likely to get out of control, particularly if violence and incivility are modeled and commonplace and there is little immediate payoff for peacefulness.

Anger comes in various forms, and emotional pain is a well-known cause for anger. Rage is the primal anger often associated with poverty, racism, and injustice. Hurt is the deep disappointment and emotional pain that occurs in broken intimate relationships and violations of personhood. Frustration occurs when habits, expectations, and creativity encounter resistance. Anxiety is a mixture of anger and fear that occurs when anger is pervasive and damaging. When expressed openly, these variations can be volatile but will usually dissipate, unless constantly stimulated by obsessive thoughts or continuing irritants. When internalized, anger becomes toxic and depressing. Such anger and variants are not uncommon in organized religion today.

NEGATIVE SOCIALIZATION

This phenomenon is the opposite of healthy, church-patterned parenting and training. It has occurred before, but previously there was often a healthy shepherding dynamic in healthy parenting that absorbed and offset its effects. Now self-centeredness, arrogance, provocativeness, negative payoffs, and violence are modeled pervasively. The point for the church is not only that we have failed in our responsibility to prevent negative socialization, but that such socialization has also infected our interpersonal relationships and behavior. Conflict has become so common that it is becoming the norm. We have not learned healthy skills for managing provocation and destructiveness.

LITIGIOUSNESS

The rule of law has long been a cultural value. In recent years, however, people have developed a taste for the adversarial approach to conflict management. This encouraged lusty growth in the number of lawyers. There may be as many as one million lawyers in the United States, for example, compared with approximately six hundred thousand physicians, five hundred thousand police officers, four hundred thousand therapists, and three hundred thousand clergy. There's a message in here somewhere!

Litigiousness has become an accepted fact of modern life, with some frightening effects and worrisome implications. Though the legal system is a cornerstone of society, it is exhibiting flaws common to other professions and institutions, such as disproportionate growth, insatiable appetites for power, and unjustified costs. The primary flaw is that the law is both reactive and prescriptive. That is, laws are typically written after a problem has developed. When laws are established in a rapidly changing society, they may already be obsolete or unjust, and yet are enforceable.

The intervention of the courts and legislatures into the affairs of the church, synagogue, and mosque is a shocking development. We must confess that it is the legal system that provided a wakeup call to malfeasant spiritual leaders, insensitive attitudes, and irresponsible practices and facilities. Thankfully, wiser legal leaders are beginning to rebuild the separation between church and state. But some lasting damage benefits have occurred. The pervasive litigiousness has encouraged high-stakes competition and incivility everywhere, including in the church. Clergy have been threatened into paranoia and avoidance tactics by lawsuits that intrude and encourage disgruntled parishioners to punish instead of work cooperatively for change.

The significant benefits have come as victims of pastoral, denominational, and congregational abuse have sometimes found the court to be an equalizing ally. However, this secular adversarial process adds impetus to contentious attitudes in the church.

"Called" vs. "Hired"

This is a crucial element of conflict and the clergy killer phenomenon in the church. Because the church as a whole has succumbed to the business model of operation, as discussed earlier, the pastor has become an employee, and parishioners the stockholders/customers. The pastor is hired to manage the small business we used to call a congregation. This means his primary task is to keep the stockholders happy; the secondary task is to produce and market an attractive product. When this mindset infects the church, the church is no longer a mission but has become a business. Parishioners and pastors agree that participants are "entitled" to a fair return on their investment; that any member can disrupt normal polity; that employment contracts and performance evaluations of only the pastor are the norm; and that evangelism is essentially a marketing effort. Because the church's tradition and polity are oriented toward spiritual discipline and mission, the introduction of a business mindset is producing dissonance in the church continually. For though businesses advocate mission and discipline, the budget is necessarily the bottom line. This is the reverse of how a healthy congregation functions.

When the church operates as a mission, the pastor is "called" rather than hired. She "serves" God first, and the denomination and congregation second. Whether parishioners "like" or "dislike" the pastor is irrelevant, for the pastor comes with an authority to nurture and lead them spiritually. Liking and disliking are the parishioners' problem, not the pastor's. Of course, the pastor is not free to rule and do whatever she wants, for she is under spiritual and ecclesiastical authority. In the same way, congregations have recourse in polity for dealing with incompetent and malfeasant pastors.

Laity are "called" also, at least in the Protestant tradition. This means they, too, must serve, not dominate. The peace, unity, and mission of the congregation is their shared responsibility. They are not required to slavishly follow the leadership of their pastor or elected leaders, but neither are they free to ignore, resist, or abuse leaders.

When the church thinks of itself as an organized mission and tries to function this way, the reference points are God's purposes, the distilled wisdom of previous and present leaders, and the Holy Spirit's dynamic guidance in their mission. Bickering, powerplays, and abuse have no place in church conflicts, of course, but the typical congregation and denomination have a long way to go in recovering the mission perspective. Massive conflicts and abuse will likely continue until it does.

With such contextual factors in mind, we are ready to examine the types of conflict and abuse that have become common in the church.

TYPES OF CONFLICT

As the church tries to develop more effective methods and polity for handling conflict, it must define conflict more carefully and develop methods for handling it that are proactive rather than reactive. In my seminars on conflict management, we examine the various types of conflict since they differ significantly and therefore, the methods used to manage them must differ significantly. In other words, the wrong medicine can make you sicker.

The three types of conflict are normal conflict, abnormal conflict, and spiritual conflict.

The definitions for these types of conflict are kept simple and obvious, for we've learned that complicated definitions and methods simply will not be learned and used, no matter how good they are. Following is an overview of the three types of conflict. Later chapters will discuss and illustrate each type more fully.

NORMAL CONFLICT

We can expect normal conflicts wherever normally functioning persons interact. We will find some degree of diversity in nearly any group, these days. Gender, ethnic, age, class, and vocational differences make it easy for people to misunderstand, fear, and therefore be in conflict with each other. It is also normal for people to disagree when they must solve problems together, since differing biases, priorities, and experiences bring different perspectives about how to handle the problems.

Personality differences also often produce conflict as each personality type tends to respond to tension and conflict in characteristic ways. Passive-aggressive personalities, for example, will likely agree to negotiated settlements of conflicts, but then sabotage the settlement by dragging their feet or raising new objections. Aggressive personalities will tend to throw tantrums or intimidate to get their way. Introverted types will tend to manipulate.

Frustrated parishioners are another source of normal conflict. These are the members who are bored, floundering, or underused or underrecognized. They may be old-timers who are unable to influence the congregation's agenda as much as they want to. They may be new members who are eager to make their mark. They may be deeply dedicated and energetic members who have not found or been given adequate outlets for service. They may be attitude-challenged members who just like to stir things up. They are not good "team players." Their behavior is usually not troublesome unless they are ignored or put down. If their needs are unattended, they are potential cohorts for clergy killers or may even become clergy killers themselves.

These normal varieties of conflict usually respond rather well to normal resolution and management tactics. Generally, we can depend on those involved to be rational and to exhibit a realistic awareness of consequences and shared needs. Relatively healthy relationships support efforts directed toward resolution.

Speed Leas offers valuable assistance in managing these normal types of conflict. His looseleaf manual, *Moving Your Church Through Conflict* (Washington, D.C.: The Alban Institute, 1992), discusses levels of conflict and how to respond.

For the more evangelically minded, James Qualben offers biblical principles for dealing with conflict. In his book, *Peace in the Parish* (San Antonio: Langmarc Publishing, 1991), the chapter "Codependency Cliques" is particularly useful in describing the conflict networks and patterns that result from family histories of addiction.

Wayne Oates brings his highly regarded pastoral counselor's perspective to the management of normal conflict in *The Care of Troublesome People* (Bethesda, MD: The Alban Institute, 1994). He describes five types of people who can make trouble in a congregation, and he tells how to both cope with them and care for them.

One of the most helpful books I have found for understanding and managing abnormal conflicts is Kenneth Haugk's *Antagonists in the Church* (Minneapolis: Augsburg Fortress Press, 1988). Haugk offers insights into personality and mental characteristics of troublesome people. He takes seriously the dangers and viciousness that disordered personalities can produce. And he offers clear advice for establishing an "anti-antagonistic environment" in the church.

A book that treats the special conflict issues of the multicultural setting is David Augsburger's *Conflict Mediation Across Cultures* (Louisville, KY: Westminster/John Knox Press, 1992). This valuable resource is one of the few books written for leaders of congregations that include recent immigrants and people with distinctive ethnic perspectives such as the role of elders, honor, and shame.

In *Managing Church Conflicts* (Louisville, KY: Westminster/John Knox Press, 1991), Hugh Halverstadt provides an elaborate system for handling normal conflicts. Though it is complicated, it offers detailed guidance for turning the conflict into a "Christian conflict." He sees congregational conflict as a problem to be solved.

The secular market is full of negotiation and mediation books that can be helpful in normal church conflicts. Books such as *The Art of Negotiating* (New York: Hawthorne Books, Inc., 1968) and *You Can Negotiate Anything* (Seacaucus, NJ: Lyle Stuart, Inc., 1980) offer methods and techniques for resolving competition, solving problems, and avoiding stalemates. We should note that negotiation and mediation models are not new nor exclusively secular. Matthew 18, Acts 15, and 1 Corinthians 12 provide biblical guidance for handling normal conflict.

While these books on church conflict are helpful, I find they are deficient in several ways. First, they assume that the pastor should lead the way and will be able to manage conflicts effectively. This is misleading in that most pastors have had little training in conflict management. This assumption is unrealistic when the pastor has become the center of conflict. Pastors who are being abused usually have their hands full with normal pastoring duties and with trying to survive the attacks. It is lay leaders of the congregation who are primarily responsible for managing conflict and abuse, according to most denominational polities. Therefore, it is a grievous mistake to assume the pastor should or can resolve most congregational conflicts alone. She can assist and even guide, but because much conflict arises out of long-standing problems, the congregation must accept responsibility for its own sin and dissension.

Most of these books also lack instruction in how personality disorders and mental illness figure into conflict. The syndromes that tend to initiate and inflame conflict are well known, and their behavior patterns are essentially predictable. It is important to factor these into any management strategy. And, it is disappointing to see that the reality and power of evil is not taken as seriously as it should be in nearly all books on this subject. It is apparent that rationality, love, and negotiating skills are inadequate for abnormal and spiritual conflicts, because their source is spiritual and human evil. Such struggles will be unmanageable without spiritual resources and methods. What follows here is a brief discussion of the additional insights and methods needed to manage abnormal and evil conflict.

ABNORMAL CONFLICT

Abnormal conflicts differ from normal ones because at least one of the participants in the conflict suffers from a major mental or personality disorder. The disorders that most commonly appear in church fights are the antisocial, borderline, paranoid and schizoid, and narcissistic personalities, as well as personalities altered from chemical abuse. These are clinical designations described in the *DSM-IV*. Such categories must not be used to discriminate and disparage, for they are not disorders of choice. They typically occur because of genetic and environmental factors, or abusive relationships. Some of the behaviors resulting from these disorders are self-generated, however, and can be modified through appropriate therapies.

Following is an abbreviated list of major characteristics (symptoms) of people suffering from personality disorders. This information comes from the *DSM-IV.*

»+ Antisocial Personality Disorder—breaks social rules, is cruel, is deceitful, is impulsive

»+ Borderline Personality Disorder—is unstable, has inappropriate and intense reactions, is irresponsible, and often is charming

»+ Paranoid Personality Disorder—is suspicious, rigid and judgmental, and vindictive

»+ Abuse Disorder (similar to Post Traumatic Stress Disorder)—is distrustful, has selective avoidance, has inappropriate guilt, uses scapegoating

These characteristics must be put in a clinical context, since normal people have these characteristics sometimes, in lesser degree, and in response to conditions in which these characteristics are appropriate. People suffering from these disorders, on the other hand, may often *appear* normal, but react abnormally or inappropriately to situations.

In the church we must be careful not to label people inappropriately, or mistreat disordered persons. But neither should we place such people in positions of authority nor try to reason and negotiate with them as if they were not disordered. The point in categorizing some conflict as abnormal is to indicate that management and resolution methods must be designed to deal with participants who are abnormal clinically and who often cannot respond in clinically normal ways. This also means some of their mental capacities are influenced negatively by their disorder. It means such disordered persons may not have a realistic awareness of consequences and shared needs. They typically do not have healthy relationships to support their efforts, or their rationality is overpowered by biochemistry.

Spiritual Conflict

The third type of conflict, spiritual conflict, differs from normal and abnormal conflict in that the instigators have an intentionally unhealthy agenda, they resort to sinful tactics without remorse, and have a persistent energy for their nefarious causes that wears good people down. Take time to review the six "D's" that distinguish clergy killers (Chapter 1).

In my judgment, we must place the clergy killer phenomenon in the evil category and manage it with intervention-type methods. Clergy killers are neither normal nor abnormal category persons. Though they may use some of the normal conflict tactics and be afflicted with some abnormal personality disorders, their predominant characteristics are those that mark persons who have given themselves to the evil agendas and tactics already mentioned.

Although conflict is a normal part of human interactions, conflicts in congregations and denominations these days are often symptoms of ill health and evil. In such cases, conflict management methods alone will not restore health. We must recognize that spiritual health ("wholeness" in the Bible) is a missing ingredient and that we need to relearn wholeness, lest we imagine we can cure pathology with aspirin. We need to learn to listen, forgive, be patient, and celebrate diversity. Yet, we must also learn to be prophetic in the biblical sense of identifying evil and fighting to rid ourselves of its influence and consequences.

Mainline churches have been caught unprepared for the increase of evil practice and ill will in congregations. In recent years mainline Protestantism and Catholicism have tended to regard sin as normal mistakes, and evil as another name for mental disorders and illnesses. This has allowed evil to gain a foothold, even among good people. And it has left us without spiritual categories and resources for handling evil.

Many religious leaders still deny the reality of evil and try to manage its consequences with tactics appropriate for normal or abnormal conflicts. The outcome is like trying to quench an electrical fire with water. The conflagration and collateral damage are increased, rather than diminished by the efforts to put the fire out.

The Bible, and Jesus in particular, takes evil very seriously. But since the Enlightenment, traditional religion has forsaken its understanding of the two spiritual realms—one good and one evil. This eliminates our best weapons for spiritual warfare, such as the forgiveness formulas, spiritual healing, discernment, and exorcism.

I am not advocating superstition, magic, and little green imps here. I am recognizing what most of our great theologians, and recently some great psychiatrists (Frankl, Tournier, Fromm, Menninger, Peck) have taught. Evil is real and powerful, and it is not expressed nor managed in purely rational ways. Conflict management methods that fail to acknowledge this will fail when applied to conflicts having evil components and agendas.

Evil is not seen as a significant ingredient in congregational conflict by many writers on the subject. We must turn to theologians who deal with this subject significantly, in order to revive our sensitivity to evil in conflict settings. Walter Wink's trilogy on principalities and powers gives us an exhaustive review of scriptural and theological conflict, violence, and abuse. This is a persuasive discussion of the spiritual perspective of congregational and world conflict. *Naming the Powers* (1984), *Unmasking the Powers* (1986), and *Engaging the Powers* (1992) (all published by Augsburg Fortress of Minneapolis) provide valuable instruction for managing spiritual conflict.

The most popular writer on the subject of evil and conflict is the psychiatrist M. Scott Peck. His *People of the Lie* (New York: Simon and Schuster, Inc., 1983) was on the best-seller lists for months. Peck gives the most concise version of the three worldviews of evil that I have found. Peck notes that the Eastern view is that good and evil are two sides of the same coin—reality. The Western view is that God created evil as a teaching resource for humankind. A shared view is that God and Satan are still fighting for supremacy, with human beings as one of their battlegrounds (see footnote on p. 46 of Peck's book). Most helpfully, Peck shows the relationship between evil and mental disorders. He also disputes the view that all people can be persuaded to behave civilly. Case studies from his practice of psychiatry give practical guidance for dealing with abnormal and spiritual conflicts.

When faced with conflict driven by negative spiritual forces and not subject to rational control, the church has shown itself to be nearly powerless recently. Jesus did not try rational solutions for evil. He gave us the exorcism formula: name the demon, cast out the demon, replace the demon with something spiritually positive. The clearest example of this three-step formula is recorded in Mark 5:1–20.

We have a similarly effective resource from the field of addiction therapy, usually called "intervention." This method has a rational basis, but it depends on interdicting the momentum of destructive behavior and thinking by surrounding it with a team powerful enough to end its dominance and lead to recovery. Vernon Johnson's book, *Intervention* (Minneapolis: Johnson Institute Books, 1986), describes this program.

In the next chapter we will discuss the differences between the exorcism model and the intervention model, and their similarities. Both models give us valuable insights for handling spiritual conflict.

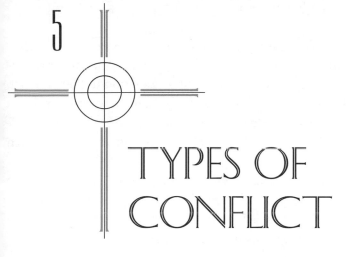

TYPES OF CONFLICT

The three types of conflict may have some common ingredients, but they require management methods appropriate to their unique characteristics, as well as a spiritually informed vision of health. This chapter provides general principles for dealing with the three basic conflict categories. Each type of conflict will be discussed in greater detail in a separate chapter.

NORMAL CONFLICT

Normal conflicts respond well to rational, competent, and caring management methods. Thus, when dealing with diversity, disagreements, personality clashes, and frustrated parishioners, an effective model of negotiation includes:

>→ Establishing ground rules
>→ Clarifying grievances and needs
>→ Speaking, listening, and giving feedback
>→ Affirming areas of agreement
>→ Brainstorming creative options
>→ Negotiating a resolution
>→ Evaluating

The variations on negotiation, namely, arbitration and mediation, offer useful options, but they usually require trained specialists. Arbitration is done by a trained or respected specialist who assesses the conflict and offers a plan for resolution. A mediator is usually a person trained to help people work out a resolution to their conflict. Negotiation may be done by nonspecialized, normally functioning persons who have a sense of fair give-and-take. If leaders are skilled and trusted, goodwill predominates in the congregation, and time is not an urgent factor, then consensus may be sought.

Consensus (when all participants agree on the proposed solution) is the most comfortable and enduring solution of all. But it is also the most difficult to achieve. Consensus is achieved by discussing conflicting issues respectfully and exploring options until all can agree.

Pastors and lay leaders may use all three of these roles, if they have the skills. But we should note that there may be legal implications in any conflict these days, and leaders are typically the targets of lawsuits. Therefore, pastors and lay leaders who are willing to lead a search for resolution should be supported in all necessary ways. The goal of normal conflict management methods is the peace, purity, and unity of the church and the fulfillment of God's purposes.

ABNORMAL CONFLICT

As noted earlier, abnormal conflicts are distinguished by the elements of mental or personality disorder. If these elements can be identified and dealt with therapeutically, then the conflict may be manageable through the negotiation models already discussed. These disorders have a strong potential for disrupting and sabotaging normal negotiations unless professional therapy is used.

There are likely to be more parishioners suffering from personality and mental disorders in a given congregation than the pastor and lay people realize, for some disorders are not apparent under normal congregational circumstances. Medications can keep some disordered people under control. Because such conditions are handled with confidentiality by therapists, no one outside the circle of confidentiality is told about the disorders and potential problems. Therefore, we need to better understand mental and personality disorders.

Pastoral counselors and other mental health professionals can be helpful to pastors and congregations who must deal with abnormal conflicts. It is not realistic to expect the average lay leader or pastor to handle conflicts involving personality disorders without professional advice. Though pastoral counselors cannot discuss a particular case, they can advise a pastor in general terms.

When dealing with abnormal conflicts in the church, the "tough love" model is appropriate. It recognizes that not all participants are functioning well, and one or more are not capable of handling the conflict rationally. The goals of managing abnormal conflict are to separate the abnormal people and factors until they can be healed, and to keep them from distorting the peace, purity, and unity of the church. The tough love model includes these ingredients:

»+ Recognize abnormal factors
»+ Clarify responsibilities for resolution
»+ Identify options and resources
»+ Strategize and select a method for negotiation or treatment
»+ Activate support systems for leaders
»+ Surround abnormal person(s) with guidance
»+ Sustain process until satisfactory resolution is reached

SPIRITUAL CONFLICT

The goal when dealing with spiritual conflict is to surround or expel the person doing evil, so that peace, purity, and unity can occur. In more conventional terms, we may use the "intervention" model, which has grown out of substance abuse therapy. Ingredients included in intervention are:

»+ Identify the crisis
»+ Build the intervention team
»+ Design the strategy
»+ Empower the team members
»+ Guide the person into disciplined recovery insistently
»+ Evaluate the process and results

Lest there be confusion, we should note that intervention is a process of imposing a therapeutic regimen on an out-of-control, destructive person whose behavior is incessantly and seriously damaging to himself or others. This is done by a team of competent, forceful persons who are willing to impose conditions that will provide recovery possibilities. Intervention is intent on ending a particular, destructive behavior. It includes treatment for the cause of this behavior and provides a disciplined lifestyle designed to prevent recurrence. It is apparent that some of the factors that make this method valuable in treating substance abuse and its consequential destructive behavior can be instructive for dealing with evil behavior.

Although intervention can be an effective tool, it is reassuring to see that spiritual disciplines (these are explained later) and theology are being taken seriously again in some conflict management models. In my seminars on conflict, we are careful to distinguish healthy spirituality from fads and cultish methods and to emphasize the value of the spiritual gift of discernment to spiritual conflict. The exorcism formula Jesus used is a valuable guide, as long as we let God's Holy Spirit lead the way.

In Mark 5:1–20 (and other places), Jesus demonstrates the three steps in exorcism. First, he named the demon(s). This naming process is powerful, because in Scripture, being able to name someone or something gives power over what is named. We cannot exorcise evil if we are unable to name it and be honest about its source and power. Second, Jesus commands the demons to leave. We can only do this with God's help, of course, but there is no cleansing unless we get rid of the evil presence and its machinations. Finally, Jesus replaces the demon with a positive message and mission. He instructs the healed man to return home and witness to his health and its source. This third step is important, for evil returns to fill the spiritual vacuum unless something positive is put in its place.

Exorcism is a formula for ending the dominance of evil in a person's life. Such a person may be inadvertently or intentionally under the dominance of evil (often called "demon possession"). Jesus spent a lot of his ministry casting out demons, so his model is primary for our instruction in dealing with evil. But evil and exorcism are frightening factors. Therefore we tend to avoid or ritualize our relationship to them, rather than allowing them to be a natural part of human spiritual experience.

The practice of exorcism has been turned into an exotic and specialized ritual in some theological circles (Roman Catholic, for example). This ritual, when practiced competently, can be helpful to people who have unintentionally come under the dominance of evil. A more common situation is occurring in churches these days when people sometimes allow their own self-centered behavior to escalate into intentional destructiveness toward God's mission in the church, and its spiritual leaders. By identifying with such an evil process, such people ally themselves with spiritual evil and its universal evil agenda. Many such people appear to enter this unholy alliance without realizing the awesome effects of their choices. Nevertheless, they then participate on the side of evil in the universal spiritual conflict between God and Satan and are drawn into its consequences.

The awesome dimensions of this struggle should not intimidate us into becoming cringing victims of evil, for the full battle is between God and Satan. We participate as underlings. Those who identify with God will tend to grow into God's positive purposes. Those who choose evil will participate in the destructiveness of evil.

When a congregation and pastor intend to end the dominance of evil in an individual's or a congregation's life, they must depend upon God's power for this agenda. Human intentions and resources are no match for the universal struggle between good and evil. Knowing that the spiritual conflict is won or lost on the basis of our spiritual loyalty (choice), however, we need not fear making this choice. And when we make it, we can have confidence that we now participate in God's power and purposes.

The point for our pastoral and congregational struggle with evil in the form of clergy killers is that we may participate in this struggle with confidence; evil does not overcome good (Romans 8:37–39, John 16:33, Romans 12:21, and 1 John 5:4). Therefore, though the ancient ritualized formula for exorcism remains valuable, it is not the only way to overcome demonically dominated persons. If we intentionally ally ourselves with God's purposes through personal and communal spiritual disciplines (see the discussion of the Spiritual Disciplines Pyramid in Chapter 13), we may confidently expect God's power to produce God's purposes in our lives and congregation in spite of evil's temporary destructiveness. We simply are faithful to God's purposes as revealed in Scripture, and we trust God to complete the exorcism. This means a church board, a pastor, or a disciplined lay person may lay claim to God's victory over evil when discerning God's purposes and identifying with them. We can trust God's purposes in patience, even when our personal agendas are not met immediately.

Pastors cannot solve congregational problems and conflicts alone. It is stimulating to see the unique opportunities that healthy spiritual leaders, including pastors, have today. It is apparent that we are called to do far more than maintain the institutional church. We are called to a mission of salvation and justice, which is now likely to include people-to-people conflict with evil incarnated.

Pastors must use great care to avoid judgmentalism, hysteria, and despair in dealing with conflicts in the congregation. The pastor is not the only possible leader in dealing with conflict, but the pastor should make sure the conflict is handled responsibly. Lay leaders share this responsibility. Whoever leads the conflict management process should be careful to maintain a facilitating role and not be drawn into the conflict as the scapegoat or fixer, for a compromised leader may become the focus and then be a victim of the conflict. A rare blend of sensitivity and caring must be combined with toughmindedness (not belligerent stubbornness) if the pastor or lay leader expects to facilitate conflict management. Discernment is the spiritual gift that makes this possible.

We should note that when religious conflicts are cross-cultural, additional resources and perspectives are typically necessary. The David Augsburger book *Conflict Mediation Across Cultures* (Louisville: Westminster/John Knox Press, 1992) is one of these resources.

Conflict management is not a once-and-for-all activity. Conflict will persist wherever human beings gather. Therefore, spiritual discipline, celebration of worship and ministry, along with training for dealing with conflict should be continuous.

N O T E S

NORMAL CONFLICT

We will now look at two cases to help identify clergy abuse and to begin thinking of solutions. An analysis follows the first case, consisting of a list of some of the mistakes made. The analysis is intended to stimulate your own analysis and action. A prescription comes next, listing significant, positive solutions to help solve the conflict.

The second case is not assessed. Use your insights and creativity to do your own assessment without the prejudice of my discussion. After reading either case through, go back and underline what you see as being significant issues. Then on the blank pages at the close of the chapter, list the mistakes and the helpful behaviors in the case. Finally, write your own comments and prescriptions for the case. After you have worked through the first case, examine my analysis and prescription. (You might rework the cases after you have read Chapter 10, "Why People Act Like They Do." There the primary roots of human behavior seen in these cases are presented.) It should be especially helpful, of course, to apply this to your own situation.

The following case fits the normal conflict category. It demonstrates how normal, expectable conflicts can escalate if they are not understood and managed effectively.

They can even escalate into clergy killer events and become spiritually destructive.

THE CASE: "MAKING LEMONADE"

Vince Lombardi, the famous former coach of the Green Bay Packers football team, once said, "If life gives you a lemon, make lemonade!" In the following case, the pastor did just that.

Cynthia Stone was a new pastor, just out of seminary. But she was not new to church leadership issues, for she had been married to a pastor whom she had divorced five years earlier. Now Cynthia was pastor of a church of her own. She was pleased with her accomplishments. She had the courage to leave a dysfunctional, abusive husband. She had gotten herself through seminary and the ordination process. And she was rearing two children caringly, even while fighting her former husband over child support and visitation rights.

Cynthia was pleased also with her congregation, at first. Even though the church was small and the town was more rustic than she would have liked, it was peaceful and, as Cynthia would say, "Heaven knows, I need some peace in my life!"

The usual welcoming process and honeymoon had occurred, and now Cynthia had settled into the weekly routine. Part of the weekly routine was meeting with the Monday lectionary group. Several local pastors met regularly to study next Sunday's Scripture lessons together. They had welcomed her self-initiated attendance.

Cynthia's routine also included visits from Angus Warbucks, who thought he was wealthier and a better farmer than he was. He also thought of himself as a leader in the church and community. His wife worked part time at the town library, giving her access to many people in town. The Warbucks had seemed friendly toward Cynthia at first, but their disapproval was becoming apparent. It was especially apparent when they came to the church office on Thursdays for coffee with the church secretary. This was the secretary's day to do the Sunday bulletin and other administrative chores. The pastor noticed that all conversation ceased when she walked past the secretary's office.

The problem was the negative comments circulating over the congregational grapevine. Cynthia heard about them through Francesca, a woman who had befriended her early on. Francesca confided that people were saying their pastor shouldn't have divorced her clergy husband, that she wasn't keeping her children under control, and that she had no business preaching about how people ought to live their lives when her life was such a mess. There was even a rumor that strange men visited the parsonage late at night.

Cynthia was devastated when she heard about this gossip, for she was working hard to be a good pastor, and the rumor about the visitors was not true. She finally asked the church board about the gossip, but the response was silence. Parishioners would talk to her on Sundays, but there was little hospitality. The overt criticism began after her Mother's Day sermon. The following week, Mr. Warbucks stopped by her office unannounced and told Cynthia he felt that for the good of the church, she should resign.

Her life became a nightmare of trying to be pastoral toward parishioners who didn't seem to want her. She asked colleagues in the lectionary group for support, but they were noncommittal. Her phone bill ballooned as she sought comfort from old friends in distant cities. She talked with her denominational executive, but the only support she got was advice to leave. Francesca seemed to be her only local friend, and even she seemed tired of the struggle.

In the loneliness of the late night, Cynthia remembered the happy, communal years at seminary. Now there was no support, and she was feeling battered and abused. Her increasing efforts to win sympathy seemed useless. She wondered why they hadn't told her about such things at seminary.

One Sunday morning she broke down while preaching. Her "emotional outburst" became the excuse the Warbucks used to rally demands for Cynthia's resignation. She gave it to them.

But this is not the end of the story. Cynthia moved back to her hometown where her parents took her in. They cared for her and the children while she attended graduate school at the university. She found a scholarship there for women who wanted to retool professionally.

Cynthia contacted me early in her graduate work, and we worked together to plan the psychological part of her study and research. Her dissertation was on how women survive the abuse that can occur in the pastoral role. She found helpful counseling during her studies, which aided her recovery, and put her pain and anger in an appropriate perspective.

I ran into Cynthia at a professional conference where I was lecturing on the abuse of spiritual leaders. She had just received her Ph.D. in psychotherapy and was happily settling into her new ministry as a pastoral counselor, specializing in the abuse of women. Already she had several pastors who were women coming to her for psychotherapy.

Case Analysis

The congregational dynamics in this case are typical, I'm sorry to say. But this woman's courage and self-management are not. This is a heartening story of how suffering can become a stepping stone for growth and responsible stewardship of our call. But mistakes were made, and these tell us what the case is all about. (Note that the sequence in which the mistakes are listed does not indicate order of importance. The numbers are for reference in group discussions.)

Mistake 1: The denomination, congregation, and this pastor did not understand the influence of unresolved issues from the past and the characteristics of this congregation. Therefore, everyone moved ahead blindly, each with their own ideas about how things should work out. This mistake is typical and will continue to be made until such unhealthy dynamics are taken seriously.

Mistake 2: The pastor did not recognize that the close relationship between the Warbucks and the church secretary needed special attention. She needed to relate closely to each in order to build better communication, and so she could diagnose correctly the negativity that was developing toward her.

Mistake 3: The Warbucks and the church secretary allowed their friendship to turn into a destructive collusion centered on their control issues and their prejudice.

Mistake 4: The parishioners, at least some of them, engaged in gossip. More sensitive and supportive parishioners, except for Francesca, did little to stop this collusion.

Mistake 5: This pastor's seminary did not prepare her adequately for what is becoming commonplace in the church, namely, incivility and abuse. Seminaries and denominational offices share the blame for not preparing and supporting pastors in these now typical situations. And they are not doing enough to prevent such abuse from continuing.

Mistake 6: Another of the pastor's mistakes was failure to go through the checklist of "stay-leave indicators." (This list will be discussed later.) This would have put the conflict and Cynthia's options in perspective and helped her either to become proactive in dealing with the prejudice and collusion issue, or to resign on her own terms.

Mistake 7: Her clergy peers made the mistake of not supporting her in her struggle. This mistake is also common among pastors who still tend to be loners. Such behavior perpetuates the unnecessary victimization of pastors left to "twist slowly in the wind" . . . alone.

CASE PRESCRIPTION

My prescription is based on the generalized method for handling normal conflicts, as presented in Chapter 5. It should be apparent that the best prescription in this case, from the pastor's side, is the prescription she wrote for herself. Cynthia turned a lemon into lemonade. She should not have been given a lemon in the first place, or at least she should have been warned about it. By becoming proactive early in the conflict, she could have shared the lemonade with the whole congregation, instead of drinking it all by herself. Following are active prescriptive ingredients.

Ingredient 1: All denominations need to find an effective way to assess congregations' strengths and weaknesses. Without such assessment this type of conflict will continue to devastate pastors and members alike, and congregations will be unsupported in their efforts to heal and grow. Because we don't consistently and accurately assess congregations, pastors must become more discerning in the call process.

Ingredient 2: Seminaries and denominational offices must take conflicts and the abuse of spiritual leaders more seriously. They share a major responsibility for screening, training, and supporting pastors. It is clear from the growing number of conflict and abuse cases that this responsibility is not being handled adequately. Thankfully, research and methods are beginning to come from both sources.

Ingredient 3: Congregations must accept their share of the responsibility for pastoral ministry (the two-way caring between pastor and parishioners) and the mission of the church. This means they must be trained and helped to develop the insights and spiritual disciplines that make shared ministry and mission possible. Kerygma and the Stephen Ministries, among others, are programmatic resources for this ingredient.

Ingredient 4: Pastors must understand the need for and the joy of caring for each other in parochial and ecumenical networks. Models for collegiality exist, and more are developing. A model called "PK Groups" will be presented later.

THE CASE: "POWERBROKER"

The deaconesses still wore their white gloves and beautiful big hats. The music was still exuberant. But the sermons, which once had the unique rhythm and authority typical to African-American pastors, were becoming weaker. Something was draining the energy of the preacher.

When Ralph Malcolm came to me for counseling, the pattern of conflict and abuse quickly became apparent. It was the ancient "I came, I saw, I conquered" motif. An aggressive CEO had joined the congregation and was attempting to displace the pastor as spiritual leader.

The Reverend Malcolm had been serving this congregation for about ten years. It had always been a dynamic community of faith, marked by economic, social, and ideological diversity. Even a few Euro-Americans attended. Parishioners had been tolerant of each other's differing views. And with Reverend Malcolm's sensitive leadership, the congregation remained stable and vigorous.

When Raymond Johnson joined the church, there was little doubt of his importance and the leadership ambitions of Marybert, his spouse. The Sunday they were received into membership, they had a beautiful after-church brunch catered for the congregation, complete with music by a small orchestra.

The following week, Reverend Malcolm was summoned to Johnson's executive office for what he assumed would be a pastoral visit. Instead, Johnson instructed him to sit down and then announced his strategy. "I expect you to have lunch with me every Wednesday at my club. There we will discuss your sermons, church finances, and any elections that are to occur. If you do not get out of line, I will support you. If you do not perform well, I'll fire you as I would any insubordinate here at my factory."

Reverend Malcolm was shocked, and said little in response. That evening he told his spouse, Madalia, what had happened. She reported a similar meeting with Marybert Johnson. They were both too stunned and frightened to do much strategizing. Reverend Malcolm indicated that he would talk to a couple of supportive board members. Madalia planned to talk to supportive friends.

True to his word, Johnson required the Wednesday lunches and reports. His instructions regarding preaching and elections became more specific. Reverend Malcolm was given little opportunity to respond. Because two board members were employed by Johnson's company, the church board meetings began to reflect Johnson's stratagems. One of these board members was chair of the nominations committee. After only one congregational election, Johnson's surrogates were on every committee.

Reverend Malcolm and his two supporters on the board decided that they wouldn't confront Johnson. They would simply wait for him to tire of his new executive game. But the game became vicious as his criticism of the pastor dominated the Wednesday lunches and was parroted by his surrogates. The women who now gushed around Marybert Johnson initiated similar attacks on Madalia Malcolm.

The Johnson-Malcolm conflict had been going on for over a year when Reverend Malcolm first appeared at my office. This appointment was precipitated by Johnson's report to Reverend Malcolm that he was in the process of bringing a well-known African-American pastor to this church to replace Malcolm. The pastor was obviously devastated as he told me his story. I referred him to a wise psychiatrist for supportive medication, and to a skilled attorney for legal advice.

Reverend Malcolm's two supportive board members were brought into the consultations. A consensus emerged in which all agreed to support and welcome the new pastor whom Johnson favored.

However, this new pastor had been an ardent admirer of Madalia Malcolm in their college years. When she and Ralph Malcolm went to visit him, he was intrigued by the opportunity to subvert Raymond Johnson's domineering and abusive strategy. He agreed to come to Reverend Malcolm's church as a secret ally to the Malcolms and loyal board members.

Dr. Cuthbart Macrorie III became the new pastor without much resistance. His first official act was to name Reverend Malcolm as copastor. This turned out to be a happy surprise for parishioners who were feeling guilty about how Malcolm had been treated, for it united the Malcolm and Johnson factions behind the pastoral duo. The congregation grew to be a dominant and ecumenical leader in the city. The Johnsons were left with few options besides supporting this development or looking inept. Raymond and Marybert Johnson left the congregation.

This case is left without analysis so that you may use it to sharpen your own skills in assessment and conflict management. You may use the following pages for this purpose.

NOTES

7

ABNORMAL CONFLICT

The following two cases demonstrate how people suffering from mental and personality disorders tend to initiate conflicts that are different from normal, and spiritual ones. Mental and personality disorders are typically not self-generated. Rather, most often they are induced by genetic flaw, trauma, illness, biochemical imbalance, or chronic negative environmental influences. Therefore, people with disorders should not be labeled and judged negatively, but should be cared for with toughminded love, assisted into therapy, dismissed from the congregation if intractable and unrepentant, and supervised closely if placed in any leadership positions.

THE CASE: "THE ABUSED ABUSER"

"I've done everything I can think of to help this woman," he said, "but she keeps attacking me as if I were the devil himself!"

He was speaking the truth. I knew this pastor personally. The church he was pastoring had an illustrious history, though the membership had shrunk. The church building was located in the oldest suburb of a major metropolitan community. The congregation and this pastor had made a special effort to minister to single parents. Its leaders were diverse. Its parishioners included retired people, some single parents, professional couples, and myriad unattached single people who worked in the city or lived on welfare. Each of the groups was represented on the church board.

The single parent the pastor was referring to worked in a clinic whose specialty was caring for troubled children. She was doing her internship there as she completed her master's degree in social work. When she had joined this congregation a couple of years before, she immediately volunteered to help with the youth program. The pastor and religious education coordinator were delighted and gave her full freedom to start any youth program she wanted. Soon she started a community Explorers Club for middle school youth. The tours she led them on and her study classes became very popular with youth and parents.

Trouble began when the religious education coordinator at the church asked her to limit her tours and class materials, for the religious education budget was exhausted by her activities before the year was half over. She was furious and went to the pastor, demanding that the RE coordinator be fired and funds be found for her ministry. The pastor was very supportive of her efforts. He called on her often in an effort to mollify her. His wife and daughter even babysat for this woman as she took night classes and worked at the clinic.

She calmed down for a while. But when it became apparent that the pastor would not fire the RE coordinator or find more money for her activities, she began to attack the pastor. First she attacked through innuendo, starting rumors that the pastor didn't care about youth ministries. Along with the insinuations, she organized the parents of her youth group to bombard the board with demands for more money for her program, and with accusations that the pastor was sabotaging her ministry.

Eventually she went to the board member who was a parent of a boy in her youth group and told the board member there was evidence the pastor was using money intended for Explorers Club for his personal expenses.

When this accusation was brought up at the board meeting, few members believed it. But because it had to do with misuse of church funds, they felt they had to investigate. When an investigation over a two-month period produced no evidence of money misused, the board voted to dismiss the claim.

At the next board meeting, the board member who had brought the charges and the woman who made the accusation showed up with a long list of charges against the pastor. He was accused of not calling on members, not being in the office when needed, starting rumors against parishioners, and so forth. The board postponed action until the next meeting.

During this time, a letter listing the claims against the pastor was sent by accusers to every parishioner. At the next board meeting, a dozen parents of youth, as well as the two accusers, appeared with the list of charges, which was now even longer. The board began to waver.

After three more months of this barrage, the board voted to dismiss the pastor. He left and took a position as interim pastor at a church in a nearby suburb. The original accuser began organizing similar attacks there, for she quickly found sympathizers when she reported to several parents in that church that the pastor had molested children in his previous congregations. The pastor was forced to leave again. He was suspended by his denomination and, at last report was driving a delivery truck.

A denominational official who told me this story said that he was finally able to get background information on this accuser. She had apparently been sexually abused as a child and never received therapy for recovery. The official thought that she made an unconscious, and therefore powerful, irrational connection between her abuse and this pastor whom she had attacked. In her mind, as a moral leader the pastor was responsible for not preventing her abuse and not punishing her abuser. Even though the pastor knew nothing about this and had obviously not been present when she was abused many years before, she blamed him. Her rage and vindictiveness were triggered when the pastor resisted her first demands to fire the RE coordinator and find more money for her program. At an unconscious level, she believed these acts showed that he would not protect her. Therefore the pastor shared blame with the incest perpetrator, and must be destroyed as punishment.

CASE ANALYSIS

Mistake 1: The congregation had no screening process for volunteer or paid leaders, as is the case in most congregations. Congregations and denominations now screen and examine clergy carefully, but the same is not yet standard for laity. Churches are so eager for volunteer help and so worried about charges of discrimination that they ignore even obvious danger signals.

Mistake 2: This woman made the mistake of not using accepted procedures for funding and planning, and by manipulating others to support her.

Mistake 3: The pastor made at least these mistakes: (a) he tried to "mollify" this woman; (b) he allowed her accusations to continue without exploring the cause of her unusual rage or insisting that she stop her accusations; (c) he did not activate his support system (he didn't really have one, except for his wife) to contain her folly and sustain himself.

Mistake 4: The board made at least these mistakes: (a) it gave her carte blanche to start any group she wanted; (b) it did not invoke the use of its official grievance procedure; (c) it did not investigate the accuser's partners in folly; (d) it allowed the focus of the conflict to shift from the woman's own mistakes to her accusations against the pastor; (e) it did not support the pastor nor the pastoral role; (f) it did not investigate this woman's background.

Mistake 5: The pastor's support system, people who saw what was happening, did not find effective ways to protect and support him.

Mistake 6: The denomination and its officials did not protect the pastor, provide outplacement, guide the board, or stop the accuser's folly and collateral damage.

CASE PRESCRIPTION

The church has a good history of ministry to people with serious and obvious mental disorders. It does not do as well with personality disorders and less obvious mental distresses, mental limitations, and behavioral disorders. Of course, neither does the rest of society. But the church and its leaders are expected to help set standards for understanding, managing, and being sensitive to such conditions. More pastors are seeking training in such matters, for most did not receive this in seminary, and they are seeing the need for it.

This case demonstrates the vulnerability of the church when it fails to detect and deal realistically with less than obvious mental disorders in its midst. The church and its clergy need not become mental health experts, but a rudimentary knowledge of mental disorders and some basic skills in awareness and in supervision (such as learning the early warning signals of a mentally disordered person headed for characteristic trouble) will prevent many church leadership problems. Many such problems derive from some kind of mental disorders, limitations, or biochemical distresses.

In this case, then, the remedial and preventative prescription calls for raising awareness of mental disorders and their effects. It calls for more careful and sensitive selection and supervision of leaders. It calls for an official and generally known complaint and distress process. And it must include improved support systems for church leaders.

We have already noted that abnormal conflicts in the church are precipitated by mental disorders, or by normal problems and conflicts intensified by mental limitations on the part of one or more participants. And we noted that negotiation is an effective method for managing normal conflicts and is often tried in the other types of conflict, with much less effectiveness. The reason negotiation is less effective in abnormal conflicts is that negotiation requires a normal rational process. Mentally disordered persons, by definition, do not have a normal rational process. Even if they participate in negotiation, they are unlikely to understand it or follow through on it.

The recommended method for managing abnormal conflict is the "tough love" method. There are several versions, but as applied to this case, the ingredients of the general guidelines presented in Chapter 5 should be adapted as follows:

Ingredient 1: Elected or appropriately designated leaders must call for the implementation of the official grievance process, and require all parishioners to use denominational and congregational polity for handling conflict. Because these processes are often limited, unknown, or inadequate for dealing with mental disorders, some thoughtful and prayerful innovation may have to take place. The strategic point is to make the situation clear enough that a consensus, or at least a voting majority, will emerge and demonstrate the need for abnormal methods to fit this abnormal situation.

This consciousness-raising process includes a sensitive and limited investigation of the accuser's life history and behavior patterns. All that is needed here is adequate indication of the mental disorder, not an exhaustive report. We must be sure that privacy is not violated nor records manipulated. Unless a member of this congregation's services can be used appropriately, such as a mental health specialist, a professional should be engaged for consultation. The knowledge and management skills needed to handle such situations are not yet commonly found.

Ingredient 2: When the diagnostic signs of the disorder are known, the tough love method described earlier can be initiated. This means the person suffering from the disorder must meet with and follow the instruction of officials and carefully selected persons who have the skills, dedication, and courage to act on behalf of the church. The mental abilities and condition of the disordered person will determine part of the strategy.

Ingredient 3: Whether a board, task force, special committee, or judicial commission, the people selected to initiate tough love need to find someone who can help them understand the abnormal conditions as well as the available options and resources. The board or other group also needs to select a plan of action and clarify specific responsibilities. They need to review their personal support systems so that no participant will be trying to handle this stress alone. And they need to cover all bases and surround the disordered person with inescapable guidance until the situation is resolved.

Ingredient 4: This prescription needs to include healing and learning ministry to those who have been hurt in the conflict. Some of the hurts may not be obvious, but the pastor and intimates, elected leaders, associates of the disordered person, and other members of the congregation are likely to need special support for a while.

The second case illustrates abnormal conflict that arises when a disordered person who has undergone therapy joins a congregation for apparently sincere motives, but whose condition hooks into prejudices and fears on the part of parishioners and precipitates inflamed, irrational reactions.

THE CASE: "PRIMAL FEAR IN ACTION"

The pastor and deacons of a small congregation had been visiting inmates in a nearby prison for years. Shortly after being released, one of these inmates, Carl, began attending worship services at this church. He came to the pastor after attending for several weeks and told the pastor he had been a child molester, but had been in therapy and was recovering. Carl said he wanted to become a member, but wanted to be open about his crime.

The pastor invited Carl to attend the new member class, where he immediately told his story. The church board accepted his membership, with the restriction that he not be allowed to work with church children. The pastor told the board he believed Carl was sincere, and the board agreed.

When he was introduced to the congregation the next Sunday, along with several other new members, Carl again told his story. The local sheriff, who was a parishioner, then rose to his feet and said in an angry voice that he would not allow this membership, for he knew what such men did to children, and if Carl joined the church, no child would be safe in this congregation. He demanded that the pastor and board rescind this membership.

When the pastor and board told the sheriff and congregation about this new member's restriction but refused to terminate his membership, the sheriff became enraged. He accused the pastor of "typical liberal naivete" and of not caring about the safety of "our children." Then he said he would call a congregational meeting very soon to tell members about the horrors of child abuse.

The next week he sent a letter insisting that all members come hear the truth about child molesters at a meeting following the morning worship service. His presentation at this meeting was an emotional mixture of fact and allegations, but it served his purpose by producing many emotional outbursts from members. The hesitant defense of Carl and his membership by a couple of board members, and the pastor's unwavering call for the congregation to "live out the forgiveness and love for all of us sinners which Jesus showed," did little to calm the meeting's mood.

In the following days, a steady stream of phone calls and office visits to the pastor were made by members who questioned his mental state as well as his pastoral leadership. Several members threatened to withdraw their pledges, and maybe leave the church. The sheriff phoned every day, threatening to circulate a petition for the pastor's removal if Carl was allowed to stay.

The board became confused and defensive. It seemed ready to let the pastor become the scapegoat. But the pastor insisted that this membership was legitimate. He called another congregational meeting and invited the denominational executive of the region to speak to this issue. This executive had promised to support the pastor and board when the pastor had phoned for advice at the time Carl first asked for membership. But she was new to the executive role, and only told the congregation that this decision was totally up to them.

So, that is the scenario. The pastor felt hurt, betrayed, and very vulnerable. He wondered whether age fifty-six was a good age to resign and seek another call.

You might wish to write your own analysis of this case, your prescription, and how this case could inform your own pastorate. The following pages are included for this purpose.

NOTES

8

SPIRITUAL CONFLICT

Spiritual conflict, as noted earlier, differs from normal and abnormal conflict in significant ways. The characteristics of normal and abnormal conflicts are often present in spiritual conflict. But there is a sense of ultimate struggle in spiritual conflict—an intuitive feeling that evil, pain, and destruction are the goal of the instigator. Although the instigator might claim other issues are the root of the problem, these issues seem somehow illusory and hard to pin down. Yet the clergy killer continues the fight, no matter what tactics of defense and resolution are tried.

We should note again that naming this category "spiritual conflict" does not imply that other church struggles do not have a spiritual component. Nor are we labeling anyone associated with the negative side of spiritual conflict as an evil person. We should distinguish among people who become inadvertent instruments of evil, people who intentionally advocate evil, and people who ally themselves with evil and thereby become one of its incarnations. But whenever healthy spiritual leaders discern that evil is present as an initiating and forceful part of the conflict, spiritual methods must be used to counteract it.

The following case is labeled "The Generic Case" because it is the original case cited to identify the clergy killer phenomenon, because so many pastors have said this describes their situation, and because it demonstrates how a seemingly normal complaint escalates through stages to become evil, and how ordinary responses and efforts to manage it fail. Though this story is told in Chapter 1, it is repeated here for ease of discussion.

THE CASE: "THE GENERIC CASE"

The first sign of the killing process began at a church board meeting. A member of the board, Tim Johnson said, "A lot of people are complaining to me about Pastor Enright. They're saying he doesn't call enough; he can't be reached when they want to talk to him; and he's not friendly enough."

Board members asked Johnson to identify "a lot of people," but he refused to name them. Then they asked for specific examples. He refused to be specific. The board said they couldn't take action unless they knew the specific complaints. Johnson replied that they had better take action, because these were important members who might leave the church.

In response to Johnson's demand, the board set up an investigative team. At the next board meeting, the team reported that they could find no tangible evidence of any problems. Johnson told them the complaints were real, and might have something to do with sexual misconduct and misuse of church funds. The investigative team did some more work, and again reported, at a later date, no tangible evidence of such misconduct. Johnson then called for a congregational meeting. This request was denied.

Before the next board meeting, a letter filled with innuendoes against the pastor was mailed to the congregation. At the meeting, the board and Pastor Enright were in a near panic. Johnson said he had talked to the bishop, and the bishop had said these were serious charges that needed to be investigated. At a later date, a new investigative team reported that there seemed to be a lot of people unhappy with the pastor. The board voted to have a delegation meet with the pastor.

The pastor was absent from the next meeting. After six months of this harassment, he was in the hospital. The board voted to send a delegation to the bishop and at a following meeting, the delegation reported that the bishop recommended removal of the pastor. By that time, the pastor was scheduled for heart bypass surgery, and it was rumored that his wife had become addicted to tranquilizers.

CASE ANALYSIS

Mistake 1: The complainant, Tim Johnson, made the mistake of not using the normal grievance process of typical denominational polity and congregational bylaws. Reading between the lines, it is apparent that he wanted to proceed on his own terms.

Mistake 2: The board began with apparent good intentions, but with no insight regarding this developing conflict. They appointed an investigative team, instead of referring to the standard grievance process. It is not a mistake to investigate, but this must be done according to polity and bylaws, with properly delegated authority, proper records and documentation, official meetings, appropriate confidentiality, and proper reports to the board.

Mistake 3: The board began to give away its authority not only by yielding to intimidation, but by failing to insist on use of the official grievance process. This told Tim Johnson that he could continue to dominate by threat. It made the board a victim rather than a savior. And it told the pastor that what should be his best and most official support (the board) was dissipating.

Mistake 4: By not stopping Johnson from escalating the attacks, the board allowed the congregation and pastor's spouse to suffer "collateral damage" (shock, confusion, guilt, anger, loss of confidence).

Mistake 5: The bishop may or may not have understood the situation, but she allowed herself to be manipulated by the complainant. Not all denominational officials have the power or the will to control conflict and perpetrators. But all have at least the moral authority to require compliance with denominational polity and theology.

Mistake 6: The board was not a pastor to the pastor, nor was the bishop. By the time the board sent a delegation to the now absent and wounded pastor, the pastor's pain and vulnerability, and collateral damage to his spouse must have been apparent. Even at this late stage the board (and bishop) could have offered supportive ministries, provided counseling resources, and sent a pastoral letter to the congregation to offset the damage from Johnson's letter.

Instead, they colluded in devastating the pastor, who could have been a helpful ally in the board's own struggle and the congregation's pain.

Mistake 7: The pastor did not exercise the authority of his pastoral office (authoritative role) and allowed himself to become the focus of the conflict.

Mistake 8: No one recognized that this had become a spiritual conflict between good and evil.

CASE PRESCRIPTION

Denominations and congregations have polities (official forms of government), bylaws (specific organizing congregational mandates), and a basic reliance on Robert's Rules of Order, not to mention spiritual disciplines (prayerfulness, toughminded love, and discernment) and common decency. There are major and minor variations in polities and bylaws from one denomination to another and from one congregation to another, but there are also some basic similarities. Such established forms of governance are uniquely valuable in managing spiritual conflict for several reasons:

»→ They grew out of past conflicts and needs.

»→ They are carefully devised, even if sometimes outdated.

»→ They guide stepwise progress toward resolution.

»→ Everyone who joins a congregation agrees to abide by them.

The following prescription is an adaptation for the generalized method for handling spiritual conflict as presented in Chapter 5.

Ingredient 1: Exorcism or intervention is the primary active ingredient in this prescription. Since exorcism is an exotic term in contemporary society and even in the church, more explanation is appropriate.

When exorcism is discussed in contemporary theology and polity, it tends to be couched in archaic language and metaphors. It is a mysterious, confusing, and even repugnant designation for many parishioners, for the church has essentially forgotten that it was born in the universal struggle between good and evil, and that this struggle is incarnated in our midst, whether we recognize it or not.

All of us need to study, discuss, and practice exorcism—the God-supported, communal, and individual effort to cast evil out of our lives. Most worship formats and liturgies contain a unison confession of some kind. In this act we name and cast out our sins. But exorcism goes a step beyond this: in it we recognize not only that we are sinners, but also that we tend, consciously and unconsciously, to allow some sinful destructiveness in our lives. We ally ourselves with evil by repetitious sinning and by harboring sympathies and collusions with evil spiritual forces.

Exorcism is our effort to cast off the bondage to evil. In this regard it is similar to conversion and sanctification. In fact, most of us believe that the spiritual transformations we call conversion and sanctification include exorcism in this general form. But because conversion and sanctification do not rid us permanently of sin and our penchant toward evil, we must practice spiritual disciplines to maintain the effect of sanctification. Periodically, most of us need renewal ("We Can Never Be Born Enough"—an Abby Press banner) to restore and nurture the growth toward spiritual maturity. Exorcism is a specific form of spiritual restoration in which evil habits and collusions with evil forces are prayerfully removed. This is believer exorcism, which can be practiced by those with an essential allegiance to spiritual health. There is no magic, no single ritual, and no comfortable, convenient way to accomplish it, for this is serious business with God, in a context of universal spiritual warfare.

I have no wish to overdramatize exorcism; there is a good reason why many believers are unfamiliar with exorcism. They do not practice it. It is not needed in most lives and faith communities where sincere faith and mission are the norm and spiritual disciplines are practiced in members' lives. This should not deceive us, however, into believing that evil is no longer a threat and that it only exists in the Hitlers of this world. When we realize the gross and continuous sinfulness of racism, greed, and injustice in so many forms, we can see the individual, institutional, even universal power and tyranny of evil. The potential and the reality of our personal participation in evil is obvious to those who can "see" (discern) in the spiritual sense.

The exorcism used in the formal rite of exorcism is different from the "exorcism" we practice on a regular basis as believers; for example, the exorcism used to eliminate evil as incarnated in a clergy killer. Exorcism here means the casting out of evil in a specific person or persons, even as they resist this. To rid itself of the evil we are calling clergy killer, the congregation must find ways either to free the clergy killer from evil or to cast the person out of the community of faith, both with God's help. Again, this is very serious business, as is the evil of abusing and killing spiritual leaders and causing the attendant collateral damage, and the exorcism of such evil. So exorcism is not proposed lightly here. It is proposed with the strong suggestion that the community of faith and spiritually disciplined pastors take time to study what exorcism is and how it works in the contemporary world. It does not work when attempted without discernment and spiritual disciplines. The first disciples discovered this to their dismay (see Matthew 17:14–21).

There are contemporary versions of exorcism in which actual demons may be cast out. I have never witnessed such an event, though I have talked with sincere exorcists who appear to be speaking of actual experiences. I am familiar with exorcism as it occurs in the confessional, in healings, in conversions and sanctifications, and at retreats where sisters and brothers in faith gather around each other in prayer and petition to assist someone in a release from a particular form of evil. And I am familiar with the disciplinary and judicial procedures in the church where evil is confronted in a person who will not repent and must be removed from office or the fellowship of the church. It is this latter version to which churches will most frequently turn for help.

Ingredient 2: Perhaps the closest parallel that we have for contemporary exorcism is the intervention model mentioned earlier. This model is effective in dealing with severe addictions and can be adapted to other severe forms of unrepentant, destructive behavior. But this must be done carefully, for it is a method developed for handling the severest of mental and spiritual problems. This method shows us how to intervene where other methods are not effective.

Intervention is a recommended method for aiding a dysfunctional and destructive person to break the pattern of destruction by getting him or her into appropriate therapy and supervision, or separated from opportunities to do damage. The basic ingredients of intervention, listed in Chapter 5, include: identify the crisis issue, build the intervention team, design the strategy, empower the team members, guide the person into disciplined recovery insistently, and then into therapeutic recovery or removal from the community of faith, and evaluate the process and results.

The team members may vary, but certain functions are needed. At least one person should be in a trusted relationship with the intervention subject so that she or he can function as an alter ego (speak for this person's feelings and interests) and still be a trustworthy advocate for getting the person into therapy or removed from opportunities to continue the destruction. There should be a person with strong financial and political power in the person's everyday life—a boss who controls the paycheck, an admired mentor, a highly respected colleague—for such power might be needed to impose or threaten needed sanctions. Specialists such as a therapist or lawyer might be needed. These people, however, may only function as consultants and not as actual team members. A pastor other than the subject's regular clergy may be needed so that the person has a trusted confessor, spiritual guide, and comforter. This team must meet prior to the intervention to become acquainted, discuss options, and develop the plan of intervention.

Preparing for an intervention includes determining why the intervention is needed, what therapy is appropriate and available, when it should begin, and how to get the person separated from the problem and his or her resistant ploys, and moving toward actual repentance, treatment, or removal from opportunities to do damage. This kind of careful planning is necessary; situations involving mental disorders are complicated but can be manageable when handled well. This plan obviously needs to include an agenda for continuing the intervention in whatever ways necessary to accomplish recovery and manageable supervision. The intervention should include a celebration of return to healthful living.

The first resort, as indicated often, is official polity and bylaws and tough-minded Christian love. Intervention is an auxiliary resource to be used with polity or when polity is inadequate. When an intervention is not possible or if it fails, then the congregation and its leaders must have the courage to follow appropriate other methods for expelling the evil in its midst. This means the person is removed from leadership offices or placed under appropriate supervision after an appropriate review or trial, as defined by polity. In the worst possible scenario, the leaders and congregation must cut off this person from membership in the congregation, for a congregation should not be sacrificed to an evil agenda.

Ingredient 3: The damage caused by a clergy killer and the stress of disciplinary proceedings or intervention cause wounds, drain energy and resources, and leave everyone stressed and somewhat confused. Therefore, the third necessary ingredient is healing.

The church has resources for healing, some of which will be helpful here. Time, shared caring, and sensitive nurture are all important. Public and private healing services and rituals may be necessary. Pastoral counseling, confessions and forgiveness, prayer, celebrating sacraments, and long cathartic conversations will be useful. The goal, of course, is recovery and return to health and mission.

Consider now a second case of spiritual conflict. This one will not be accompanied by analysis or prescriptions.

THE CASE: "THE GARBED KILLER"

Sam Miller didn't look like a clergy killer, but then, most of them don't. (It's important for us to develop a new mental image in organized religion. Many religious people still find it hard to believe the church can include a person, particularly a highly placed leader, who is determined to destroy pastors.) Sam Miller was a suave, handsome man with a "command presence" about him. People noticed him when he entered a room and paid attention to his well-modulated baritone voice. In fact, if you didn't notice him, he was aware of this and found a way to gain your attention and elicit a respectful response. He always wore clergy garb. In fact, one of the comments made behind his back by peers was that he probably had a cross embroidered on his undershorts!

In spite of this pontifical style, however, Miller was not stuffy or unapproachable. In fact, he often regaled groups with clergy humor and stories. He made a point of looking people in the eye and drawing out of them life stories, or at least some report on what was happening in their lives. And he remembered. The next time he talked with you, he pointedly commented on something you had told him about your life.

Such an affable and affirming style served Sam Miller well in his role as bishop, as it had served him during his several pastorates. He had devoted followers everywhere he had been. Only a few knew about the victims of his quiet, vindictive rage and predatory sexuality. But once you saw through the facade, the sociopathic pattern was evident to those willing to see and understand.

One of his victims was a beloved middle-aged Italian pastor who had served the denomination well and was now senior pastor of a large, thriving metropolitan church. On the first Sunday after the clergy killer was elected bishop, Miller came to the pastor's church early, before the first worship service, and told the pastor that he, the bishop, intended to preach the sermon at each of that day's services. The pastor was shocked and refused to allow this. The bishop became enraged and shouted, "I am your bishop. You will do as I say!" But again the pastor refused. And the bishop said, "You will rue this day!"

From that day on, Miller found ways to spread innuendos and derogatory stories about this pastor and his family. When the pastor tried to tell people the truth about what had happened between the bishop and himself, no one would believe him.

Within a year, the bishop had rounded up support for his demand that this pastor take early retirement and never serve a church again. The pastor is now retired, with a stigma attached to his name.

A few courageous leaders finally blew the whistle on this clergy killer. A sheriff and a pastoral counselor, wise in the ways of sociopaths and perpetrators, teamed with a couple of well-known pastors to lay the case before the national bishop. After long, careful investigation, this clergy killer was defrocked and paid penalties. However, Miller still maintains his innocence and will tell all who listen that the church defrauded and betrayed him.

KILLER CLERGY

It is distressing and sad to write about pastors who have failed. Yet, clergy are not honest if they do not accept responsibility for the good and the bad among them and accept the limitations of their humanness. I have written and spoken often about the noble qualities and faithful stewardship of most pastors. In fact, I consider myself an advocate for clergy and an ambassador of competent spiritual leadership. But advocacy requires honesty.

We should note at the outset that according to my research and that of my colleagues, there are fewer killer clergy than clergy killers. Most clergy killers are lay people. Killer clergy typically are clergy persons who by definition are dependent on the church for vocational and financial support. Therefore, it makes little sense for clergy to be destructive in the church, while laity do not have the same vested interests unless they are seriously incompetent, have personality disorders, or have allowed themselves to become agents of evil.

THE CASE: "KILLER PASTOR"

The first information I had on this case came from a lay leader attending one of my seminars on problems and opportunities in spiritual leadership. Louisa Palermo caught me at a coffee break and asked if I would tell her if something was wrong with her pastor. As I listened, she blurted out a list of behaviors that apparently had been troubling her and other parishioners for a while. Her troubled face and sincere, nonvindictive attitude were my first reassurances that this was not a clergy killer at work on a pastor.

Louisa reported that Pastor Gilmont seldom called on church members, even when there was trouble that indicated the need for pastoral attention. Then when the church board asked why he didn't call, he would tell them he had been under heavy pressure during that time. When the board asked him to do a particular task or wondered why a pastoral task wasn't done, he would turn on his charm and assure them that everything was under control.

Louisa's list of concerns included Pastor Gilmont's inappropriate humor. Apparently, he played the clown a lot. But his insensitive teasing and embarrassing efforts to turn most conversation into humor gave an impression of insincerity.

Louisa said Pastor Gilmont was considerably overweight and a slovenly dresser. It was becoming known around town that he was careless about paying bills. He often "lost" his car expense vouchers and receipts, and yet demanded to be paid for these expenses. It was difficult to contact him, for he frequently did not return phone calls. Nobody seemed to know what he did with his time. He was late for meetings often, and sometimes didn't show up at all.

The most serious concern was Pastor Gilmont's spiritual leadership. Louisa said members were tired of hearing approximately the same sermon over and over. His Bible classes were poorly prepared. And some members reported that when they sought pastoral counsel, he was flippant and insensitive with his advice.

When I asked how long these behavior patterns had been occurring, Louisa responded that Gilmont had been like that ever since he came, about three years earlier. People had liked him at first and saw him as a refreshing change from his stodgy predecessor. But his style wore thin, and active members began to leave. He was affable, easy to talk to, and his informal style was comfortable. But reality set in as serious deficiencies became apparent.

When I asked what had been done to address these issues, Louisa said the church board had repeatedly tried to help him correct problems. Three board members had resigned, and two left the church. Other veteran members reported trying to help Gilmont make changes, but were rebuffed. At least one told of being ordered out of the church office with loud epithets. A growing number of members gave up and joined other congregations.

This woman and her family had begun attending church elsewhere after she visited with Pastor Gilmont's denominational official. She said she made an appointment with the official, even though it entailed a long drive to another town. She said she told him in a kindly way that people were not criticizing or trying to get rid of Pastor Gilmont. They sincerely wanted to help him become the pastor they needed. It was plain to her, however, that the visit would not produce beneficial results when the official responded critically. He ushered her to the office door with the comment that he hoped she could find a different church home more to her liking. (Most denominational officials are not so insensitive and protective of destructive pastors. They are often a good resource for clarifying and managing such difficult situations.)

CASE ANALYSIS

Mental disorder may have played a part in this case. Because I did not work with this pastor in a therapeutic setting, I cannot offer a precise clinical assessment. But because I have worked with many pastors, some who were incompetent and some who were killer clergy, I can offer a basic analysis.

Pastor Gilmont may have had one of several personality disorders, as classified by the *DSM-IV*. The classification schizoid personality includes some characteristics exhibited by this pastor, including his resistance to close relationships, solitary lifestyle, and indifference to criticism and helping efforts. He also exhibits some characteristics found in the antisocial personality disorder, such as failure to conform to normal behavior patterns, deceitfulness, irritability and aggressiveness, impulsiveness, consistent irresponsibility, lack of guilt and remorse, and a long-standing history of such behavior. Characteristics of the borderline personality disorder are present, as well, in unstable relationships, impulsive eating and spending, ambiguous identity and behavior patterns, lack of empathy, and emotional instability. The mood disorder called dysthymic disorder (depression) may be indicated by the overeating, low energy, apathy, inappropriate humor, low self-esteem, and poor decision making. The bipolar disorders are also a possible diagnosis.

If any of these disorders are present and operative, clinical treatment, including psychotherapy and medication, will be necessary for improvement. Patience, reasoning, and negotiation are not likely to be effective, even though they may seem to help temporarily. If any hidden addictions (substance abuse) are present, treatment specific for the addiction must be included.

The reason we should rule out normal behavioral failures and incompetence in this case is because of Pastor Gilmont's persistent pattern of destructive behavior, the ineffectiveness of normal caring efforts, and unwillingness or inability to achieve positive change. The one-sidedness of efforts to bring improvement and change (the pastor didn't initiate efforts for dialogue or improvement) is a significant indicator. The Palermos were left with few options besides supporting this development or looking inept. The haunting presence of destructive behavior in other aspects of this pastor's life indicate the seriousness of the disorders.

We should note that the presence of irritability, insensitivity, inappropriate humor, overweight, occasional tardiness, and lack of some pastoral skills are not indicators of mental-emotional disorders in themselves. Most normal people exhibit such behaviors occasionally and may exhibit one or two persistently. It is the long-standing, intractable clusters of destructive behavior that suggest a clinical diagnosis.

Most pastors do not suffer from clinical disorders. They may have unwanted habits, lack some social skills, and have personality clashes with parishioners. These are normal, even if unpleasant, behaviors. Typically the behaviors can be modified or eliminated with normal supportive efforts on the part of both pastor and parishioners. Though pastors can be expected to exhibit social skills and professionally appropriate self-management, we all should remember that spiritual leaders are human. This is not an excuse for incompetence and insensitivity; it is simply a reminder of reality and its implications for interpersonal relationships.

Research indicates that approximately 2–4 percent of pastors are incompetent for the responsibilities of the pastoral role. A similar percentage suffer from one or more mental disorders. Though this percentage of disorder is less than that of the general public, such incompetence and disorders are more costly and damaging when they occur in spiritual leaders.

Because neither laity nor clergy readily think of pastors as having the same mental problems and emotional proclivities as other human beings, it is important to rethink our idealization of the clergy role and the human beings serving in this role. We must teach ourselves to watch for early warning signals, understand appropriate therapies, and do preventive maintenance on clergy as well as lay people, for a mentally or emotionally disordered pastor can be deadly to a congregation, community, and denomination.

Evil clergy are a rarity, but they certainly exist. Just as lay people may ally themselves with evil, consciously or subconsciously, so may a clergy person. However, it is relatively rare to encounter an evil clergy person because most denominations have training and evaluation processes that adequately screen out evil practitioners.

The Bible gives us some insight concerning this issue. Some spiritual leaders of the Older Testament became instruments of evil. It appears that prophets were expected to point out evil leaders. Such prophets often were not taken seriously, and they were likely to be attacked when they accused someone of evil. Jesus in his prophetic role called evil spiritual leaders "false shepherds" and warned of their destructiveness.

These conditions exist today, and the prophet who has discernment and courage and is willing to point out evil spiritual leaders still risks serious repercussions. The spiritual power of the forces of evil can be awesome. Individuals and congregations who trust an evil pastor can be spiritually devastated as he wreaks destruction.

Just as we pointed out the characteristics of mentally disordered clergy, so we note those that distinguish evil clergy. First, they are against life and wholeness, no matter what their claims. Evil clergy purposely reverse or interfere with the health of the church, even though they may camouflage their behavior.

Second, evil clergy are deceitful—intentionally. This is one of the hallmarks of evil. It means that the evil ones are likely to use camouflage—"blowing smoke," adopting ingratiating behavior, dissembling, denying, manipulating, and accusing others—to distract from their own tactics. It is sometimes hard to believe how an affable or seemingly dedicated pastor can be so destructive, until we step back and notice what is really happening in her or his ministry.

Third, evil pastors have a persistent, destructive agenda. Just as mental disorders are marked by the persistence and destructiveness of the illness symptoms, so the behavior of evil pastors is consistently evil, even though they may seem to be doing pastoral activities. One way of becoming aware of an evil pastor is to notice how often we must excuse his behavior and its effects because they do not conform to the pastoral norm. As mentioned, evil pastors may camouflage their destructiveness with affability. They may, however, make little effort to mask their evilness. A few seem to dare any-one to blow the whistle on them. But most stay in power because they know how to survive politically, and they trust that the inertia of congregations and denominational offices will work in their favor.

Fourth, killer pastors know how to attract and organize followers for their unhealthy purposes. Occasionally, an evil pastor is a loner. It is more likely that killer clergy will have dupes or equally evil cohorts.

Fifth, it will likely be the more mature and discerning spiritual leaders of the congregation who will sense this presence of evil and warn against it, or at least have trouble accepting and cooperating with evil killer clergy. It fol-lows that healthy spiritual leaders are seen as deadly enemies by evil killer clergy, and therefore are typically targeted for criticism and abuse by them.

Pastor Gilmont "killed" this congregation in several ways. He reversed its natural tendencies to nurture and reach out in mission. He did this by not doing these things himself, and by not encouraging and nurturing such efforts in parishioners.

Pastor Gilmont killed the congregation with confusion and frustration. The people were accustomed to following their spiritual leader, but he didn't lead. They expected to share the leadership, but without clear communica-tion from him, they were confused about what their share was.

Pastor Gilmont killed the congregation by generating anger in the members. His habits, his lack of communication, and his poor sermons and pastoral ministries angered them. They paid an adequate salary and benefits and were eager to love and support him, but he rebuffed their efforts. Few parishioners will give generously to a church with this kind of pastoral leadership.

The congregation slowly began to show its frustration and anger by leaving or by contributing less. Income dropped substantially. With loss of spiritual energy, loss of substantial members, and loss of income, the death of the congregation had begun.

Obviously the life and health of the congregation shouldn't depend solely on the functioning of the pastor. But a pastor like this makes it extremely difficult for a few loyal parishioners to keep the church alive. It should be just as obvious that the reason the pastor is called and paid is because of the need for a reliable, nurturing professional to function as symbolic and actual guide for the communal spiritual pilgrimage. When the pastor is incompetent and destructive, the people are cheated of the anchor for the leadership team.

Clergy have a unique responsibility to help eliminate evil pastors. At the same time, clergy must recognize the likely consequences of such prophetic behavior. Equally important is the caution that a pastor who is stubborn, insensitive, and even incompetent is not necessarily evil or mentally disordered. Our responsibility is to help eliminate intentionally destructive pastors.

Harmful clergy are the largest category of killer clergy. They are simply harmful or toxic to a congregation. The harmful ones are those who cause more harm than good in their attempts at ministry. They may be sincerely mistaken, immaturely self-serving, or professionally incompetent.

Pastors who are toxic to the congregations they serve are misfits. Their personality, style, and convictions do not fit the needs or the personality, style, and convictions of a particular congregation. The congregation and denomination share the responsibility for spiritual leadership, so blaming incompatibility solely on the pastor is not sensible or responsible. The congregation even promises to accept the pastor's leadership at the installation service. Therefore, it has a responsibility to be accepting and adapt its expectations as long as it is receiving reasonable pastoral leadership. But we are not discussing reasonableness and responsible behavior here. We are recognizing that a few pastors do not fit a congregation's needs and are unlikely to, even when the congregation is adaptable.

The church is getting better at identifying harmful and toxic pastors. Career development centers that specialize in evaluating clergy are doing a valuable service by identifying these killer clergy and recommending training, treatment, or outplacement. A certified pastoral counselor or chaplain may also serve this function. Secular mental health professionals are sometimes not able to conduct such evaluation, for many do not understand how competent and incompetent spiritual leadership in the church is exhibited in everyday practice.

MANAGING THE KILLER CLERGY PHENOMENON

Once the church admits the reality of killer clergy and understands this phenomenon, management issues become clearer. Therefore, we must study issues of incompetence and destructiveness among pastors more carefully. We cannot assume that ordination produces healthy leaders.

For mentally or emotionally disordered pastors, therapy, supervisory support, or outplacement with therapy and vocational retooling are appropriate.

For evil clergy, intervention, exorcism, and spiritual supervision are necessary.

For harmful clergy, a blended prescription is often needed. A sensitive yet toughminded assessment of the destructive behavior by mentally and spiritually healthy leaders of the congregation and denomination is required. It may be necessary to provide vocational retooling, therapy, and strict accountability. And it is likely that long-term mentoring will be needed.

We should remind ourselves, the congregation, and denominational officials, however, that as surely as there are dysfunctional clergy, there are dysfunctional lay leaders—and more of them. Laity often contribute to the dysfunction of destructive pastors by allowing the destruction to continue or by participating in it. Though we must improve our efforts to identify and manage killer clergy, we will not produce healthy congregations until destructive laity are managed better, as well. Training courses and adult forums on healthy spiritual leadership are available and certainly should be used in many congregations. Laity who are biblically illiterate, spiritually undisciplined, and uninformed about congregational polity are likely to be incompetent and perhaps destructive leaders. Pastors, even incompetent and evil ones, should not be scapegoats for destructive and incompetent laity.

We should note here that the responsibility of denominational leaders in dealing with killer clergy is heavy. They must be astute in recognizing killer clergy, assessing the congregation, and suggesting remedies. Denominational leaders are not only vulnerable to criticism for their efforts, but they are also now legally vulnerable. Pastors must learn how to be more supportive of competent denominational officials.

The best strategy for handling the killer clergy phenomenon is prevention, of course. The problem lies in not seeing the needs and not meeting them appropriately. In the case of killer clergy, however, we need to be more specific. Denominational polity and the congregation's bylaws provide some remedies for handling killer pastors. Following these closely may eliminate the problem. They certainly provide the safest guidelines in a day of recriminations and legal vulnerabilities. Specialized clergy, such as pastoral counselors, chaplains, seminary professors, ordained lawyers, and the like may provide the strongest assistance. Prayer can also be effective. Where none of these work or are available, leaders might need to depend on eventual resolution through a combination of polity, patient prayer, and innovative strategies such as positive incentives or close supervision to neutralize an evil pastor's influence. Offers of attractive severance packages may also effect helpful change.

The roles of spiritual leaders are changing, as are other forms of leadership. The Bible and church history show what happens when the community of faith does not require accountability from its leaders and does not support them adequately in their leadership efforts. Our world obviously needs effective spiritual leaders. It is the church's responsibility to identify dysfunctional spiritual leaders, to deal with them appropriately, and at the same time to support competent leaders effectively.

10

WHY PEOPLE ACT LIKE THEY DO

This chapter serves as a basic resource for understanding human motivations and behavior in general. Its purpose is to demonstrate the inner workings of the human mind, because the clergy killer phenomenon does not occur in a vacuum or accidentally. It grows out of basic motivations in the service of negative or evil perspectives on life, or a particular event.

One of the questions we often find ourselves asking is, "Why do people act like they do?" Related questions such as, "How can she do that?" "Why are they doing this to me?" or "What in the world would make him act like that?" also reflect our feelings of anger, hurt, amusement, or curiosity. When we are under a clergy killer attack, such questions demand answers.

It is normal to wish we better understood human behavior—our own, as well as that of other people. Human work, play, and relationships require that we make some assumptions about human motivations, but we are often wrong. Life experience gives us clues, but this is a slow and imprecise way to learn. Therefore, we seek reliable information to guide our suppositions. If we wish to improve the quality of human life and relationships, it is mandatory that we find better models for understanding human behavior. This is especially true for those who lead others. Pop psychology, sociology, science, and the Bible give us major clues about behavior, but we still have trouble translating the explanations into helpful tools.

We ask such questions for a variety of reasons. One reason is self-protection, which is certainly primary when clergy killers attack. If I can predict what another person will do, and its effects on me, perhaps I can avoid more pain and disappointment.

Another motivation is manipulation. If I can anticipate the others' responses to my actions and needs, I will more likely be able to control them. Leaders are motivated by the need to succeed, to lead effectively, or to move people toward goals. This tends to encourage both unhealthy and healthy manipulation.

Pastors are likely to ask why people behave as they do based on all these and other motivations. But there is little question that most of us would be better pastors if we understood the motivations and needs of other people and ourselves more fully.

Because the question of human motivation has been asked for so long, there is an abundance of data and speculation that can inform us. Unfortunately, many of the insights from the past were biased or just plain wrong. For example, people commonly believed that women could not be strong leaders, that African Americans were inherently less intelligent and less motivated than whites, that men shouldn't cry, that children couldn't understand sexuality, that pedophiles can be cured, that those who have different religious beliefs than ours cannot be trusted, and that clergy killers are only misguided parishioners.

Some valuable insights from past psychological and theological systems still inform our understandings of human motivations, however, for ours is not the first generation to think great thoughts about the world and humankind. The problem for most of us is finding time to select, read, and understand the past masters. In an effort to understand human motivations and in lieu of formal study, it is common for pastors to select a couple of masters to read and then to blend these insights with their personal and pastoral experiences.

Here I offer a model I have developed through years of study and ministry as a pastoral psychotherapist.

AGENDAS FOR HUMAN BEHAVIOR

Early in my pastoral counseling with pastors, I saw a need for a simplified version of relevant insights from theology and psychology. I took the risk of trying to distill these insights into a simplified model that would be of service to spiritual leaders. I call this model "Agendas for Human Behavior." This simple diagram provides a visual reference.

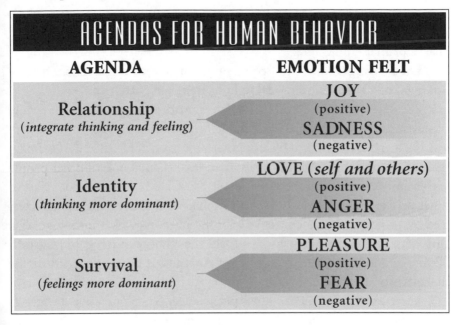

AGENDAS FOR HUMAN BEHAVIOR	
AGENDA	**EMOTION FELT**
Relationship (*integrate thinking and feeling*)	JOY (positive) SADNESS (negative)
Identity (*thinking more dominant*)	LOVE (*self and others*) (positive) ANGER (negative)
Survival (*feelings more dominant*)	PLEASURE (positive) FEAR (negative)

Academics call such a model a theoretical construct, a theory about a set of facts of data. Caveats must accompany such a theoretical construct, of course, for a perfect distillation of the masters is not possible. Further, when we find an attractive simplified model of complicated formulations, we might be tempted to embrace and use it indiscriminately. Finally, because each human being's and group's experience is unique in some ways, no one model exhausts experience. But a model provides some guidance and encourages us to further study human motivation, for religion and its practice cannot be understood without a coherent sense of human motivations. Make use of this model where it is helpful, and lay it aside when it is not.

Following are some general principles that inform the "Agendas for Human Behavior" model.

1. Basic patterns are observable in human behavior. Because so much in these patterns is repeated across ethnic, gender, age, and class boundaries, we may assume a primary, shared motivation for each.

2. Though there are infinite variations on these patterns (agendas), we can assume that both unconscious motivations and conscious intentions combine to generate what we will call an agenda, for we can see the evidence of both the conscious and the unconscious in our behavior and that of others.

3. The agendas are basic to individual, group, and organizational behavior. Although they are not exhaustive of human motivations, they are reliable as primary indicators.

4. The three agendas are not equal in potency or consequences. They are arranged in a hierarchical model to indicate relative strength.

5. The agendas are not discrete (isolated entities). They ebb and flow and blend, and yet each remains identifiable, with a unique goal.

6. Each agenda is marked by a singular objective, here called the "primary issue." This objective takes the form of an open-ended question. An agenda is primarily expressed in the ways people motivated by this agenda relate to other people. We call this the "law of relating." And each agenda is characterized by two emotions, one positive and one negative, which form a polarity that acts like electricity, which impels the energy driving the agenda. "Positive" and "negative" are not judgmental terms here. They identify the biochemistry of the emotions.

7. A feature of the agendas is their persistence. When operative, an agenda demands our primary attention and maximum energy resources. It remains dominant until its concern is satisfied. This process will be examined more closely later.

8. There are normal pressures on this hierarchy of agendas. The most powerful human emotions are characteristic of the more primitive agendas—survival and identity. Although nearly all of us pursue the relational agenda, it is the most tentative of the three. Discipline and concerted effort are required to move ourselves or a group to this agenda and sustain cooperative behavior.

9. Life stages, present circumstances, and habits (tradition, socialization, and coping mechanisms) all affect but do not alter the agenda's basic function.

10. For those of us who take religious faith and the gospel seriously, it is apparent that individual and communal faith provide answers to the question of each agenda. Faith also gives coherence to this whole model, which

expresses the image of God in each of us, and calls us to responsible participation in God's purposes in creation. This model is offered here in terms
common to both psychology and theology.

THE SURVIVAL AGENDA

This is the original, foundational agenda for human beings. It arises from
the primitive, animal-like parts of our brain. This agenda does not make us
animals, but its motivation and intentions are the least rational and most
potent. It is important to understand the survival agenda in relation to
clergy killers, for clergy killer attacks force everyone to function and think
based on this agenda.

The survival agenda is the one we start with every day and is present in
most of our behavior and thinking, unless we learn ways to modify this normal tendency. When trying to understand our own behavior, we should
assume we are functioning with this agenda, unless we see and feel clear evidence of another agenda. And we should assume that other people have this
same tendency.

As noted, each agenda has a clear and simple primary issue, a familiar and
yet typically unconscious question. The survival agenda's issue is, "Am I safe
here?" This is not a casual question; it is the survival question. Though it
seems self-centered, it is the most important question in life to any of us. At
its best, this question usually keeps us from risking too much and keeps us
alert to danger. At its worst, it generates exaggerated fears, conflicts, aggression, and paranoia.

It is important to note the potency not only of this agenda, but also of the
many forms it can assume. For example, we may learn how to deny our fears
while appearing calm. We may camouflage our behavior behind a smile
while trying to destroy a perceived enemy. And we may become sensually
indulgent in an effort to calm our fears.

The emotions that mark this agenda are fear and pleasure. Note the negative-
positive polarity, for this is a highly energized agenda. Fear is the most powerful of all human emotions. When fear is triggered, it overrides any other
emotion. Pleasure is nearly as powerful, and in the addictive-compulsive
disorders, it can balance and even overpower some fears.

Because we tend to worry about these two emotions, we tend to mask or
deny them. Think about a familiar scene such as two children denying their

fear and trying to taunt each other into being the first one to dive into the deep end of a swimming pool. It is not necessary to be quivering, sweating, or cowering in order to express our fear. We may also bluster, threaten, or become coolly calculating or vindictive. We may even develop a foolhardy bravado or become ingratiating toward frightening enemies we perceive as powerful.

Pleasure also takes a variety of forms, from the grossly sensual to the elegant rituals of sophisticates. There is little doubt of the power of physical-emotional-spiritual pleasure. Not everyone finds the same things pleasurable, but all are serious seekers of pleasure. We may even develop negative tastes, such as sadism, vindictiveness, and pursuit of some forms of pain, and come to experience these as pleasurable.

The polarity of these two emotions is instructive, for we may play one off against the other. Fear is often used to curb the excesses of pleasure. Likewise, pleasure in various forms can assuage fear. Thus, some serious addictions and compulsive behaviors are generated.

The law of relating that dominates the survival agenda is the law of the jungle—"I get you before you get me" or "You have your turf and I have mine" or "An eye for an eye and a tooth for a tooth." In its civilized form, this law is expressed as "live and let live." Though such motivations can be camouflaged, a perceptive eye can note the power and consequences of this agenda.

This original agenda persists until its primary question is answered satisfactorily and behavior that is not focused on survival is learned. People cannot be convinced to abandon the agenda through scolding, threats, or punishment. It does not even yield to moral or ethical messages such as "Thou shalt not kill," or "We should all be kind to each other," or "You shouldn't drink so much." Such messages, though good in themselves, do not break through this agenda unless they actually respond to the primary issue that drives them. Unless they deal with the primary issue, these moral and ethical messages only postpone or deny the inevitable outcomes.

For the person who wishes to move herself off this agenda or to assist others in doing so, the effective method is to answer the survival question in ways that make sense to the person on this agenda, because this agenda tends to cancel out or override any other data except realistic assurance of safety and comfort. This is important for the church and for pastors to understand. If we do not honor the basic question of safety and address the need for safety, people with this survival agenda will not find the ministry they need in this church or from this pastor.

When the appropriate answer is provided, however, a person on the survival agenda is freed to move to a higher agenda. This is a remarkable transition for people whose lives have been dominated by fear and pleasure. Such freedom does not come easily. The message that we are safe and will survive must be powerful and attractive enough to retain power over idiosyncratic fears and pleasures. Any of us can have our fears and appetites triggered by familiar or new cues, in spite of New Year's resolutions. So freedom from the dominance of the negatives of the survival agenda is always tentative and must be reinforced and guarded. We are never fully free from the survival agenda except through delusion, euphoria, or ignorance. But this agenda is not all bad. It keeps us alive, protects our interests, and helps us understand others.

THE IDENTITY AGENDA

When freed from immediate survival needs, a person typically encounters the full force of the next higher agenda—the identity agenda. Though less potent than the survival agenda, this one has similar dynamics. Therefore we may discuss it more briefly, focusing on its uniqueness.

The primary issue of this agenda is, "Who am I?" A corollary question is, "What difference do I make here?" This too is a powerful question, one around which some people focus their lives. In its negative forms, the response to the question leads to narcissism, selfishness, and pride. Its positive forms lead to self-consciously healthy ways; awareness of the image of God within, gifts, and talents; awareness of weaknesses; and a sense of stewardship of self.

It is important to note that when a clergy killer attack begins, a pastor is likely to experience the attack in the realm of this agenda. Therefore, the attack feels like and is interpreted as a violation of personhood. It is normal then to feel anger. And it is normal to react to the clergy killer as if their interaction is a contest of wills. As the clergy killer attacks continue and intensify, however, we crash down to the survival agenda. Fear overrides other emotions and the law of the jungle becomes operative.

The emotions that mark the identity agenda are anger and love. Both are powerful and can be manipulated for self-serving purposes. Though these emotions seem familiar, we need to learn their subtle characteristics, because they are basic expressions of our personality. What makes us angry and what we love are a major part of our identity. We are angered when we feel our personhood is violated or ignored. And we feel and express love when our personhood is respected and affirmed.

Anger, like fear and pleasure, is a basic emotion. We are born with it. We have no choice about having these three emotions when they are triggered. But we do have a choice about how to manage them. Herein lies one of the tasks of maturity.

Love, on the other hand, is a learned emotion. We are born with a potential for love, but not with love itself. We need to experience caring love and to see models of it if we are to become loving people.

Because we are continually learning, people who have not learned love by experiencing it and having positive models in formative years are likely to learn to express their potential for love in negative forms such as codependency, dominance, and narcissism. This is why the church must continue to enact the love dramas of life, as well as preach love, for admonitions and words about love are meaningless unless a person feels and sees love.

The law of relating for this agenda is the law of competition. This has familiar forms that can be positive as well as negative. Humans do not compete healthfully and for healthy goals unless they feel respected and believe that the goals are honorable.

This agenda, as the survival agenda, has a preoccupation with self. One of the unique characteristics of the identity agenda is its focus on individuality. This has both positive and negative possibilities. We have already mentioned the good possibilities: awareness of the image of God within us; development of gifts and talents; and the stewardship of self. Because these characteristics are typically appreciated by others, we tend to be more conscious of them. These can be tainted, however, if we flaunt them or imagine we are better than we are.

The negative potential of this agenda needs some extra attention because it is typically unconscious (hidden from ourselves, at least) and tends to drain energy from efforts to develop the good potential. The Bible and theology give us valuable insights into this dark side of ourselves. But because we have all been influenced by popularized versions of serious psychology, it will be useful to review briefly the contributions of several clinicians concerning our negative potential and motivations.

Carl Jung's concept of the "shadow" self has gained ascendancy in recent years. With this shadow metaphor, Jung tells us that we have another dimension to our selves, a companion self. Largely unconscious, this self is the aggregate of our unknown or unwanted characteristics. Other people may or may not see our shadows, and we seldom see this shadow ourselves, because it is largely unwanted and therefore denied. The effect of denial, as we have learned, is to allow us to ignore what we don't like.

This shadow self is nearly as powerful as our acceptable, public selves, and in some situations it is even more powerful. It tends to be self-centered and self-serving. It throws tantrums when it doesn't get its way; it manipulates people; it is judgmental of others, and uses its own interests as the reference point in decision making. One of its favorite tactics is projection—deflecting attention from its own faults to others, usually by accusing them of the faults the shadow self is trying to hide. Such projection is one of the most difficult dynamics to manage in the self and in interpersonal relationships, because we are unconscious that we are doing it, we are by definition diverting attention from ourselves and we often cause angry reactions in those onto whom we project.

Sigmund Freud taught us about the power of our unconscious. One aspect of our unconscious self is a process called introjection. This means incorporating into our own behavior or beliefs those of a beloved or hated person or object. We are deeply influenced by our remembered experience, real or imagined, of this person or object. In circumstances that trigger such memories, we tend to react under the influence of those memories, rather than dealing with the situation according to present reality.

More recently, proponents of what is called object relations theory have developed a detailed scenario for identifying and tracing the development and influence of this dynamic in our lives. This is a valuable perspective that is becoming popular among pastoral counselors and other mental health professionals. Two recommended resources are *Dictionary of Pastoral Care and Counseling*, Rodney J. Hunter, ed. (Nashville: Abingdon Press, 1990), and *Self and Others* by N. Gregory Hamilton (Northvale, NJ: Jason Aronson, Inc., 1990).

William Glasser expanded the idea of how we are influenced by our models into a way of understanding why some people's lives develop negatively and remain negative. He taught that individuals and society become self-centered in bad ways when they lose connection with healthy communal goals and healthy people. Such losses leave individuals and society under the dominance of self-centeredness, with all its potential for good and bad. People with bad histories will live these out, to the detriment of all. Glasser's writings have been valuable for years, and two are still recommended reading: *Reality Therapy* (New York: Harper & Row, Publishers, 1965) and *The Identity Society* (New York: Harper & Row, Publishers, 1972).

The good aspects of our selfhood, already mentioned, can be enhanced and empowered by God's Holy Spirit, just as our bad aspects may be empowered by evil. It is reassuring to know that not only is our Creator the source of our talents and gifts and the image of God within us, but also that God offers power to invigorate our good potential and control the bad. A particularly focused version of this power is what we term the "call," or our conviction that God's purposes are functioning in our lives to stimulate our motivations toward good goals. It is particularly reassuring to know about and be able to open ourselves to such power when we are up against negative motivations and the power of evil.

The point of paying attention to the good and bad aspects of our unconscious selves is to remind ourselves and each other that much of what occurs inside, and between us, comes from unconscious motivations. We are limited in positive development if we do not learn to identify and manage our shadow traits and potentialities. Clergy killers, for example, may be unaware of or insensitive to their motivations. And the targeted pastor may be unaware of how or why her or his own thinking and behavior contribute to the victimization.

THE RELATIONSHIP AGENDA

This most cherished of agendas has dynamics similar to the other two, but its attitude and behavior are significantly different. The self is central to the others, but community is primary to this one. It cannot be achieved without first answering the characteristic questions of the prior agendas. Pastors expect to function with this agenda and expect to lead others to it. However, when clergy killer attacks occur, this agenda is only a fond memory or hope.

The primary issue here is "What's in it for us together?" This means we are open to each other's needs, talents, and perspectives. In fact, we pay attention to these and look for ways to express caring, even as we learn the value and power of synergy and community. With this agenda, differences are enriching, disagreements are negotiated, and a satisfying dynamic of give and take is developed.

The law of relating that prevails is mutuality—one for all and all for one. Individual expressions are encouraged and critiqued in love. Priorities emerge through consensus, and resources are shared in thoughtful stewardship.

The emotions that mark this agenda are learned, as love is. Sadness is the deep sorrow that occurs when relationships fail. Joy is the enormously exhilarating satisfaction that occurs with mutuality.

This idealized yet realistic agenda is very tentative. Threatening and egotistical behavior and cues can instantly draw our attention and energy to either or both of the prior agendas. It doesn't take much negative pressure to push all participants down to a survival agenda. But when the questions and answers and positive behaviors are attended to and supported, the relational agenda can be reached quickly again. In fact, healthy individuals and groups learn quick and effective ways to move toward the relationship agenda, even under pressure.

It should be obvious that this model is not exhaustive of human behavior, and that it has strengths and weaknesses. But it offers some helpful tools for understanding, growth, and mutuality by distilling the enormous insights of many great thinkers, therapists, and spiritual leaders.

The primary purpose of this model is to answer our continuous and pleading questions about why people act as they do—why I act the way I do. Because this is a key question for pastoral ministry, studying these agendas for human behavior can simplify and bless many ministries.

MOTIVATIONS THAT DRIVE HUMAN BEHAVIOR

Beyond the model just presented are a host of motivations and intentions which drive human behavior. Most of these are matters of choice, whether conscious or unconscious. From a theological perspective, we must also assume that a sovereign God can intervene in the agendas already operative as a result of God's act of creation. We also assume God has universal purposes beyond our individual needs. If we accept the traditional theologies, we must acknowledge a negative power at work in our midst as well. We will return to the positive purposes of God later. Evil needs our attention here, for this is power beyond our human control, even as God is beyond our control.

EVIL AND GO(O)D AS MOTIVATION

Since this book is not a formal theological treatise, concepts and references have been kept simple, even though they deserve broader discussion. The purpose here is to note spiritual designs beyond our full comprehension and control, for they certainly influence human behavior.

Contemporary mainline theology has neglected evil. It has become common to develop concepts such as injustice, oppression, poverty, mental disorders, and a host of "isms," such as racism and sexism, as ways of accounting for evil in our world and in ourselves. These negative concepts certainly have basis in everyday life, but they do not exhaust the meaning and functioning of evil.

If we could find ways to overcome racism, sexism, and the like, we would not have rid the world of evil. If we were able to feed and treat everyone fairly, we would not have rid the world of evil. And if we were able to heal mental disorders, we would still not have eliminated evil. All of these conquests together would bring us closer to having the kingdom of God on earth, but until spiritual powers resolve their conflict, we will always be influenced by them in known and unknown ways. The term "sin" itself connects our flawed human motivations and the designs of evil, for sin is about our individual and corporate failures. It is also evidence of the presence and influence of evil.

Though the analogy is not perfect, we may use magnetism as a metaphor for evil. Magnetism here refers to the familiar force by which a magnet attracts metal. A piece of steel is pulled toward a magnet by this unseen force, and the closer the piece of steel gets to the magnet, the stronger the pull. If the piece of steel is drawn into the force field of the magnet in the absence of another power that resists this pull, the steel is finally pulled right up against the magnet. Though it still looks like the original piece of steel, it is now attached to the magnet and may become magnetized itself.

By applying this metaphor to our motivations, we can say that evil influences all of us in some ways. People who allow themselves to be attracted to evil are in danger of being pulled into full contact with evil, which results in their becoming dominated by it, even while appearing to remain the same person.

Because mainline Protestants, as well as others, have discarded the concept of evil, we are no longer prepared to recognize or cope with it effectively. We find ourselves unable to manage effectively people and influences that have become agents of evil in our communities and churches because we are using ineffective methods and tools. Our puny efforts are like trying to stop a military tank by throwing rocks at it.

The phenomenon of clergy killers destroying pastors is an example of the power of evil overcoming our normal human defenses. Remember that elsewhere we have described clergy killers as relentless destroyers, empowered by evil, who target moral leaders (usually pastors) for destruction. Repeatedly I see cases of conflicted congregations and their pastors unable to deal with clergy killers effectively because they are using the wrong methods: being nice to clergy killers, trying to mollify them, and trying to negotiate with them.

All of these methods are helpful in dealing with normal conflict. But they do not work against evil. People who are dominated by evil are not transformed by even our sincere human methods any more than a tank is stopped by people throwing rocks. Rock-throwers stand helpless before the oncoming tank and will be crushed by it, unless there is intervention by another friendly, overpowering force. When clergy killers are suffering from personality or mental disorders, signs of the presence of evil in the world, the dominance of their disorder will not yield to kindness or appeasement. This must be accomplished by therapy. In the case of clergy killers, we learn to do interventions to isolate and disable them and to develop healthy congregations and clergy who are "street smart" about evil and empowered by God.

Turning our attention to the good spiritual force we know as God, we note much more familiar characteristics. And yet, for all this familiarity, we have not defined God nor brought God under our control. The mystery of God is power, energy, beauty, and goodness beyond our comprehension. But we believe, through God's revelation, that God is for us (see Romans 8:31, 37–39), and thus we may depend on and even become agents of God's purposes and power, even as others become agents of evil.

Magnetic force remains a useful analogy for understanding the power of God. Just as we may become attracted to evil and allow ourselves to be drawn into its power, we may do the same with God. We must allow ourselves to become attracted to God, and then we must learn spiritual disciplines in order to become agents of God's grace and people who live under the power of God.

The goodness and grace of God include what we have come to call tough love, for God is in a war against evil. Those who identify with God are therefore in this conflict. We tend to enjoy and be comforted by the niceness and caring in our Christian understanding of God. The forces of evil are capable of manipulating us into believing that everything in the church should be comforting and peaceful. When we are thus seduced, we become vulnerable to evil and unprepared for the hard work of resisting it. We may even blame God for our discomfort and battle wounds, or imagine something is wrong with us when we are traumatized.

Slowly the church is learning (again) that in order to battle evil we must toughen ourselves spiritually and learn to discern evil and its influences. This means we must open ourselves to God's gift of discernment (often called understanding, wisdom, or interpretation in the Bible—1 Kings 3:9; Ecclesiastes 9:13–17; Malachi 3:18; 1 Corinthians 2:14 and 12:10; 1 John 4:1). Then we must learn how to align ourselves with God's purposes.

Not all human weaknesses and conflicts are the result of evil. Things such as ignorance, prejudice, ill will, mental disorders, and conflicts can be accounted for through normal human functioning. For example, not all people in a congregation who have conflicts with their pastor are clergy killers. In fact, most are not. Diversity, disagreements, and personality clashes are normal and expectable events. These can be managed (not always easily) by our sincere efforts to listen, understand, care, and negotiate.

The differences between good and evil are not as apparent and easy to identify as we might imagine. It is easy, as we have all noted in ourselves and each other, to judge as evil (or at least bad) anything we don't like. Thus, we tend to demonize some other people and fight them as if we were doing God's work against evil. Actually, in most cases, we are only demanding our own way and imagining that this is God's way.

Many are beginning to realize that good and evil are real, that we must identify with one or the other after learning to discern the difference, and that we must "grow in grace" if we are to becomes agents of God in the struggle against evil. The power by which we are motivated is the power to which we have made a commitment. Clergy killers are allied to evil and this is why they have extraordinary power to destroy. Those who ally themselves with God can thereby draw on the extraordinary power of God to overcome evil.

MENTAL DISORDER AS MOTIVATION

Mental disorders have been mentioned several times in this book. I have found that though pastors may be familiar with them and even discuss them, there is a continuing need for more information. So a few more basics are offered here.

Mental disorders are breakdowns or genetic flaws in the healthy, normal functioning of the human brain. Using the *Diagnostic and Statistical Manual of Mental Disorders, Fourth Edition (DSM-IV)* developed by the American Psychiatric Association, we note many such disorders which influence human behavior through distorted motivations. Some motivations are influenced negatively by disease, genetics, peer pressures, trauma, and the like. Some have relatively benign effects while others are destructive. We cannot begin to examine all the disorders here, but several are selected because of the difficulties they add to church conflicts in general, as well as the clergy killer phenomenon.

One of these is antisocial personality disorder, popularly called sociopathic personality. This disorder is marked by a pervasive pattern of disregard for the rights and needs of others, exhibited in failure to conform to social norms, deceitfulness, impulsivity, aggressiveness, irresponsibility, and lack of remorse. Closely related to this disorder is the borderline personality disorder. It is marked by instability in relationships, identity, and moods. The unstable moods may include inappropriate displays of anger and hostile aggression.

Such disorders contribute to confusion and contention in the church because they can be masked. (Not all disorders can be masked.) Or, the disordered person might be misunderstood as simply "difficult to work with." The conflict may be viewed as normal dissension arising from diversity, disagreements, personality clashes, and boredom. But human idiosyncrasies and differences are quite different from mental disorders. The first two typically respond to social norms and interactions in manageable ways. People with the mentioned mental disorders are unpredictable and likely to become malicious. If people afflicted by mental disorders are allowed to take leadership, they are likely to handle it in irresponsible ways.

The abuse of clergy is often led by a person with antisocial or borderline personality disorders who has consciously or unconsciously aligned herself or himself with evil. Disordered people are particularly capable of manipulating naive or other disordered persons into following their pathological agenda.

This does not mean, of course, that all obstreperous or uncivil persons are mentally disordered. We must be able to distinguish the difficult from the disordered in order to relate to them wisely and pastorally.

A tragic and painful psychic trauma is important to our discussion. Physical, emotional, and sexual abuse of children and adults appears to be a growing phenomenon—or at least we are becoming more aware of it. We are also just beginning to learn the devastation and lingering effects of abuse. The abuse we are discussing here is the undeserved and inescapable kind perpetrated on vulnerable children and adults.

The abuse of a child in particular not only violates the rights and health of the child, it is likely to affect negatively this child's interpersonal relationships all through life if there is no therapeutic intervention. When that abused child grows up, if he or she becomes a member of a church, it is unlikely that any parishioners, and often the pastor, will know about or understand the effects of the abuse. We may not, therefore, minister to such an adult appropriately or be alert to the difficulties he or she may have relating in the congregation. If the abused person also has an antisocial or borderline personality disorder, a volatile mix is created. Let us examine again the example used in Chapter 7, "The Abused Abuser."

The abused or mentally disordered adult may focus blame and therefore malevolent behavior on the pastor or other moral leader, for such a person is unconsciously seeking someone to blame for the devastating emotional pain suffered. Because the abuse was undeserved, inflicted, and damaging, this person rightly sees it as a moral issue since morality is about good and bad behavior. By implication, the pastor, who is an identified moral leader, should have prevented or stopped the abuse, even though the pastor was not there during the abuse. The nonrational connections of childhood come into play here and persist in an unconscious way into adulthood. This is how a pastor is sometimes targeted for abuse and even destruction by an abused or mentally disordered person.

We should remember that such a person can hide the abuse and mask the disorder. The person can even be ingratiating and appear near normal when relating to the pastor and parishioners—until the unconscious agenda of retribution is triggered by an unintended slight, a misinterpreted response, or disappointing behavior. Then a pernicious pattern of behavior begins that will not cease until the pastor is destroyed or removed.

We should also remember that such people do not respond appropriately to behaviors such as kindness, listening, mollifying, and negotiating. The disordered or abused person's agenda is not deterred by these behaviors the way a normal person's would be. Therefore, it is important to recognize such people and situations so that we can manage them better and minister to such victims and survivors in more appropriate ways.

Such people are not fully responsible for their abuse or their disorders, for they may be incapable of other choices. But the consequences of their behavior must become the responsibility of all who care in the church. We must love them in ways appropriate to their conditions. This means they must be identified early and channeled into treatment, if at all possible. They must not be allowed to harm others or acquire leadership positions until treatment has been effective. And if they begin their pattern of devastation, they must be stopped for everyone's benefit.

It may be helpful to note here the significant similarities between disorders traceable to childhood abuse and what is now called post-traumatic stress disorder (PTSD). This syndrome was brought to our attention by some of the abused and traumatized veterans of the Korean and Vietnam conflicts. It is not uncommon for an adult abused as a child to experience and exhibit the feelings and behaviors symptomatic of PTSD. Both groups of people may have painful flashbacks, use extraordinary means to avoid experiences, objects, or people who trigger traumatic memories, and they may be unstable and unpredictable at times.

Another disorder is based on substance abuse. Church leaders and members have learned many of the characteristics and dangers of this disorder. Because there are many such abusers among parishioners and pastors, church folks need to continue to pay attention to this disorder, for its sufferers and the consequences often contribute to church contentions and the clergy killer phenomenon.

We have discussed the more damaging and disabling mental disorders, but not all people with mental disorders are strange or incompetent or dangerous. And all deserve the informed care and understanding of the church. No one is without flaws, weaknesses, and sin, so we must develop our consciousness of these disabilities in humility and love.

The church is becoming more aware of the effects of mental disorders and pastors are being trained to minister to disordered people more effectively.

But our denominational polities and traditional thinking in parishes often are out of touch with such realities. The consequences of misunderstanding them is traumatizing many pastors and draining the resources of the church. We are missing opportunities for appropriate ministries to such people.

BIOCHEMICAL MOTIVATIONS

As we learn more about ourselves as human organisms, we are realizing that the biochemistry of our bodies is a powerful influence on our behavior, whether we are aware of it or not. Because our physical bodies are sustained by chemical reactions taking place inside of us, our bodies tend to be dominated by such biochemical activities. Therefore urges produced by hormones, endorphins, enzymes, and such will control our behavior unless we learn how to manage these rationally and healthfully.

One of the new fields of biochemistry is chronobiology, the study of the biochemical rhythms, cycles, and stages that occur in the human body. Circadian rhythms are one example of biochemical fluctuations. Circadian rhythms complete a cycle of fluctuations within twenty-four hours. Our blood pressure follows a circadian rhythm, typically going through a predictable high and low phase each day.

Other biochemical effects are driven by such volatile chemicals as adrenaline, testosterone, and progesterone. Though we cannot see these and other chemicals coursing through our bodies, they account for a significant proportion of our attention and behavior.

Most of us are aware that our physical energy varies also, typically reaching highs early in the day and early evening, with lows midday and during the night. These can all be influenced by other rhythms and outside agents. When we learn to identify and respond to such rhythms, our lives feel more comfortable than when we try to resist or override them.

Given our bodies' hundreds of biochemical rhythms, cycles, and stages, as well as their interactions and responses to outside influences, wise self-management suggests we become aware of them, for they certainly influence our behavior. We also need to become more aware of the individual differences in such biochemical fluctuations, since not everyone is being influenced by the same biochemistry at a given time. We also must recognize the larger rhythms of all creation. We live with the influences and consequences of each other's rhythms and reactions, so it is folly to ignore them.

There are many more motivations and intentions that drive human behavior. The ones discussed here may serve to stimulate more study, and more self-conscious management of ourselves and our institutions. And they certainly help us understand the clergy killer phenomenon.

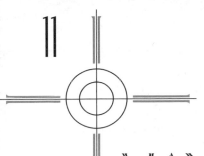

MANAGING THE CLERGY KILLER PHENOMENON

I t has taken awhile for denominational and congregational leaders to recognize the reality of intentional, destructive attacks on pastors. This means we must teach ourselves the skills needed to survive these attacks. All the pastoral protection and abuse prevention issues discussed in this book seem unlikely to become urgent agenda for others until we make them so for ourselves and those we hold dear.

This is not an "us versus them" game to be played in congregations and denominations. It is a fact of life for pastors; it "goes with the territory." You may not have encountered clergy killers in your ministry, but it is likely you will one day. Or you might know colleagues who have encountered clergy killers and have the scars to prove it! The point is that the clergy killer phenomenon is our issue, and will continue to be even after the church understands and is more supportive. Therefore, we must learn how to protect ourselves, how to be toughminded regarding these issues, how to network for solutions, how to heal and grow, and how to help build healthy congregations. These issues were introduced in Chapter 3 on collateral damage. The remaining chapters cover them more thoroughly.

Some humor may be helpful as we begin to address the personal issues in managing the clergy killer phenomenon. This gallows humor, offers a laugh to lighten what is often a painful experience. The following list is obviously for laughs, not for serious consideration!

Clergy Survival Kit
1. Mace, cattle prod, grenade
2. Night-vision binoculars
3. Karate handbook
4. Gifts for appeasement: a pound of your flesh; a pint of your blood; a resignation letter (in disappearing ink!)
5. High barnyard boots (it gets deep!)
6. Decoding ring (to see truth!)
7. Mine detector
8. Ferocious Halloween mask
9. Beeper (for support group)
10. Prayer beads

In seminars on the clergy killer phenomenon, we often take a little time to laugh over this list of survival tools. Typically, some jokes are shared, such as:

When a clergy person falls down the stairs, the Catholic will exclaim, "Well, I deserved it as punishment for my sins." The Methodist will pray, "Lord, help me to understand this event and become a better person having lived through it." The Presbyterian will say, "Well, since it had to happen, I'm glad it's over." The Baptist will cry out, "Which of my deacons pushed me?"

Another joke goes like this: Three little boys were arguing over whose dad was the richest. One said, "My dad is the richest, 'cuz he owns the biggest farm in the county." Another said, "That's nothin', my dad owns the biggest bank in town." Then they both turned to the third boy and said, "Bet your dad doesn't own anything, 'cuz he's a preacher." "Oh yeah," the preacher's kid replied, "My dad owns something bigger than a farm or a bank. He owns hell." The other boys laughed and said, "That's ridiculous. How do you know your dad owns hell?" The boy replied, "When my dad came home from church last night, I heard him tell Mom that the elders gave him hell!"

The research and anecdotal records of how humor aids in coping with pain and in healing has become impressive. Norman Cousins' encouraging book, *Anatomy of an Illness as Perceived by the Patient* (New York: W.W. Norton Co., Inc. 1979), was an early leader in the pop healing field. Physicians, psychologists, and assorted researchers have reinforced the use of humor and positive entertainment to facilitate healing and recovery, as well as a way to promote health. Similar use of the arts and meditation have long provided a hospitable setting for healing and health.

Humor and lightheartedness are notoriously difficult for clergy. The professional role seems to require solemnity, dignity, decorum, and piousness, all of which by definition exclude humor. Yet we learn in pastoral ministry that these must be balanced in our professional and personal lives for our own health, and for credibility in our professional lives.

When we are depressed, hurting, anxious, and confused, humor and lightheartedness aid in releasing us from anxiety, pain, and hopelessness. When intimidated and traumatized by serious conflict and the onslaughts of clergy killers and their cohorts, it is often worthwhile to intentionally add some humor and entertainment to our lives. Humor should not be used so heavily that it becomes a form of denial, avoidance, or addictive coping. Rather, it should be used to balance the heaviness of life, and as a stimulus for hope and creativity.

SURVIVAL SKILLS FOR CLERGY

Because clergy killers typically target clergy (or perhaps another authority figure in the church), they had better learn survival skills. This seems incongruous, for pastors tend to think that because their role and intentions are so noble, no one will attack them. But pastors must come to terms with diversity and critics, and learn how to negotiate differences. Pastors must learn survival skills, for they may encounter clergy killers. And if they do, noble intentions, Christian love, and negotiation will not save them. Even if pastors are willing to sacrifice themselves, they share responsibility for defending congregations, because clergy killers are perfectly willing to destroy congregations in their efforts to destroy pastors.

It's often called "street smarts." I'm referring to the know-how needed by those who live and work in areas where extreme danger from other human beings is prevalent. Such awareness and skills are distant from the typical training and experience of clergy, unless they have worked in dangerous neighborhoods. Therefore our starting place is a new perspective, a different kind of awareness.

Those who live in large metropolitan areas have learned to do things they don't want to do in order to be safer and help protect themselves and others. Car keys aren't left in the ignition anymore. People don't travel alone in certain places after dark. They even avoid giving personal information over the phone.

Pastors should take the idea of street smarts seriously, not as an attitude or way of life but as a way to raise consciousness of how the world of hostile-aggressive people (street gangs, terrorists, clergy killers) really operates. Gang members cite the following ingredients as necessary for survival on the streets.

1. Believe someone wants to kill you!
2. Stay "cool"—think!
3. Know street rules
4. Keep yourself strong
5. Prepare safe places for hiding and support
6. Develop strong allies
7. Know danger signals
8. Know your enemy
9. Know your limits
10. Have a plan (plan A, plan B, plan C, etc.)

Survival skills for clergy begin with changing thought patterns. Here are some examples.

1. Believe that it is possible for someone to want to destroy you.
2. Understand that your denomination typically has little power or inclination to save you from clergy killers.
3. Learn the danger signals and patterns of behavior of clergy killers (see the six "D's" discussed in Chapter 1).
4. Be aware that proaction is far better than reaction in dealing with clergy killers.
5. Learn that building relationships in the congregation is key to preventing clergy killer attacks and provides a protective synergy. It is also good pastoring.
6. Accept the fact of evil and mental disorder in the church.
7. Expect the attacks of clergy killers to have serious negative effects on your congregation and loved ones. Therefore, your survival skills are also important for their protection and should be taught to them as well.

8. Learn that awareness and survival skills need not produce paranoia, nor rob you of the joy of ministry. They simply aid you to
function in ways appropriate to contemporary reality.

Think with me for a few minutes about these eight factors. Even though
they are self-evident, most of us have to think and rethink them so they will
become part of our professional repertory.

The notion that someone—a parishioner—may want to destroy a pastor
is probably astonishing, but it's true. I can cite many cases across denominational lines. Perhaps you can too. In military training, soldiers are
reminded over and over that the enemy's purpose is to kill or disable them.
We learn that even if certain foods or medicines are attractively packaged and
advertised, they still may be seriously harmful. We know that wild animals are
never fully domesticated and are likely to turn on us, no matter how kindly
we treat them. "Nice churchgoing folks" can be out to get you, too.

The fact that denominational officers often have little power or inclination to rescue pastors when they come under serious attack is usually a
shock to new pastors. Such officials may even collude in their destruction.
Most denominational officials are well intentioned, but they are also vulnerable. The reality is that they may need pastors as much as pastors need
them on occasion. This does not mean pastors should avoid denominational relationships or become loners. Rather, pastors must learn the realities of what to expect from their denomination.

One of the most helpful insights is that clergy killers give signals and
operate in patterns. The signals and patterns can help us recognize that our
assumptions that clergy killers are normal parishioners is wrong. Pastors
must shift to a different way of functioning when dealing with clergy killers.
When pastors pick up the signals and note the patterns, they must then
empower themselves to act with a different than normal agenda, for normal
pastoral behavior is not effective with clergy killers.

The fourth necessary change in thinking is to take the initiative when
dealing with clergy killers. If pastors remain reactive, the clergy killers' persistence is likely to wear them (or their supporters) down. Most pastors pre-
fer to wait for consensus or assume clergy killers will quit. Neither of these
is likely to occur. Therefore, the suggestions listed later in this chapter under
"Skills for Congregations" and "Skills for Denominations" should be factored into a pastor's proactive strategy.

The fifth valuable strategy is building relationships. Just as real estate agents say the three keys to a valuable property are "location, location, and location," so we are relearning that the keys to healthy pastoring and self-protection are relationships, relationships, and relationships.

Some pastors tend to build a "palace guard," a group of favored parishioners. Some pastors develop a jovial approach to members that is intended to make them feel noticed, and yet holds them at a distance. Some pastors cultivate close relationships with the powerbrokers in the congregation for obvious reasons. And some pastors limit their relationships to compatible parishioners. Such relationships may be comfortable or useful, but they are not the key to healthy pastoring.

The relationships that both affirm members and support the pastoral role are the ones built upon consistent contact, that respond to each other's needs, and are related to the mission of the congregation. This should include a growing number of parishioners as the pastor's tenure increases. It should also include a cross section of the membership. Support for the pastoral role and the person in it will be a natural byproduct of this growing network of positive relationships.

The pastor must build relationships with people with whom she has personality clashes and people who are potentially troublesome. Regular pastoral contact with such people can soothe irritations early, can help the pastor understand how such people function, and can provide a positive model for the congregation.

Building relationships seems like hard work to shy and private types of pastors. But healthy pastoring and personal survival depend upon it. Once a pastor realizes this, a relational pattern of pastoring can be developed that gradually removes the stress of doing something that feels unnatural. Such relational pastoring is an antidote to the lonerism that afflicts so many pastors.

Sixth on the list of survival skills is a working knowledge of evil and mental illness and disorder, which often is missing from our arsenal of defenses when we deal with clergy killers in the church. Though pastors may know evil and mental disorders exist, they may not associate insights about them with clergy killers until too late. Because clergy killers usually appear to be relatively normal adults, pastors tend to miss negative, telltale data. And because pastors tend to believe the myth that Christian love conquers all, they fail to deal with clergy killers in ways appropriate for evil and mental disorders. They need to remind themselves often of the insidious abilities of clergy killers to camouflage their intentions and to enlist normal but naive cohorts. In order to develop skills for handling clergy killers, pastors must study evil and mental disorders; they will not avoid injury unless they understand these. Normal strategies of patience, love, consensus, courtesy, and cooperation are ineffective. Tough love works.

In my experience, the wakeup call for a pastor under attack by a clergy killer comes when he sees injury to loved ones and the congregation. The thinking of clergy killers resembles military officers who are willing to destroy a village in order to save it from the enemy. Clergy killers pay little attention to collateral damage when pursuing their destructive goals.

Finally, the pastor with this new awareness should not become paranoid, for this hands a victory to clergy killers by default. Neither should pastors allow themselves to lose the spiritual disciplines that keep their vision of ministry clear and allow them to savor faithful ministry. Good survival skills are hampered by paranoia and self-imposed martyrdom. (Self-imposed martyrdom here means forcing yourself to do more than the ministry situation requires.)

Following is a list of additional resources and skills that can contribute to a personal strategy for your situation.

1. **Personal support system.** For many years I and others have been advocating and teaching upgraded clergy support systems, for traditional ways of supporting pastors often do not meet contemporary needs. Spiritual leaders are beginning to learn that they are responsible for their own health. Having a personal support base is critical to survival of clergy killer attacks.

2. **Personal health management.** Energy and its management is another resource and skill critical to healthy pastoring, whether a pastor is under attack or not. Physical, emotional, and spiritual energy is a limited and precious resource. We all have a lot to learn about this human resource. Clergy killers can distract pastors into dissipating their energies into hopeless worry and fighting.

3. **Professional competence.** Excellence in ministry is a noble and satisfying goal. Pastors are more vulnerable to clergy killers and to loss of support and failure when they fail to learn and grow and improve.

4. **Professional consultants.** Pastors are not alone in their struggles with clergy killers. There are professional resources and people—lawyers, pastoral counselors, mentors, and so forth—who can help. When pastors are

unaccustomed to using such resources, we must learn what many others learn in times of deep distress: you are only alone if you choose to be.

5. **Continuing education.** Finally, pastors don't learn all they need to learn about ministry in seminary. No seminary produces perfect pastors. Continuing education and growth must be formulated to expand perspective and skills. Part of the problem with clergy killers occurs because pastors haven't learned how to deal with diversity, dissent, and conflict.

Before turning to skills needed by congregations and denominational offices, we need to note the unsavory reality that a few pastors not only resist dealing realistically with conflict in their congregations, but they also want to suffer or be victimized. This may be a conscious or unconscious motivation. Either way, it is patently an unhealthy one. Such pastors need therapy. They obviously will be unable to deal with conflict realistically, either on their own behalf or on behalf of the congregation.

It is a serious matter to find a pastor who savors his own suffering. So the needs of such a pastor must be distinguished from those who complain a lot, or who have trouble coping with abuse. The pastor who relishes her own victimization characteristically has a previous pattern of such behavior. It is likely that she will collude in her own suffering by emphasizing her mistakes, defending her abusers, and featuring her pain. On the other hand, pastors who are simply suffering great pain and confusion, and having trouble coping with it, are more likely to seek relief, show anger at abusers, and be debilitated by the abuse. Not all pastors experience and handle abuse in the same ways. The differences can be significant.

FIRST AID

When pastors are traumatized and hurting badly, it is normal to feel confused about what is going on and what to do about it. It is also normal to have much less energy available to think clearly about options and strategies. Let us focus, then, on the simplest guidelines emerging from study of the suffering and recovery of battered pastors. The guidelines are listed, and a discussion of them follows.

1. Recognize and assess personal wounds
2. Recognize the need for help
3. Assess collateral damage

4. Identify types of conflict and abuse and remedies
5. Apply appropriate remedies
6. Review personal options and decisions
7. Facilitate healing and health

These are general guidelines covering conflict, abuse, damage, and recovery. A battered pastor (along with injured intimates) must personalize them. This is not selfishness nor dereliction of pastoral responsibilities; rather, it is good stewardship, for if the pastor is destroyed, the whole congregation suffers, and the perpetrators win.

Recognizing and assessing personal wounds is not as simple as it may seem. The mental process called denial is a real possibility, especially for "macho" types or for pastors who believe that clergy shouldn't be wounded in the church. Because such injuries are usually mental, they are not visible, except for some symptoms. It can be a shock to really see your wounds and realize the trauma. Most of us need a "mirror" and assistance from others to understand the damage and be honest about the effects. Recognizing the personal need for help is often complicated by the "oughts" and "shoulds" in our minds, just as assessing wounds is. This is another reason to reach out for help from your support system and from other available resources.

The most immediate need, of course, is to stop the "hemorrhaging." Using the physical model here, we recognize that if much blood is lost, shock and organic breakdown occur quickly. Mental hemorrhaging is not as obvious nor immediately terminal, but it is, nevertheless, life threatening in the sense that rationality is impaired, which means behavior may become counterproductive, which in turn means irreparable damage may ultimately occur.

Here is where a therapist and trusted friends become important. During the shock of wounds and trauma it is normal for a pastor to need someone to listen as she assesses her own thought processes, and to offer help for what she cannot do for herself. In this step pastors need to deal with the "Why?" question, to accept and manage the feelings of outrage and violation, to reassure themselves that they are not alone in this mess, and to explore their personal faith issues, including the forgiveness dilemma. Also among the faith issues is the possibility that their suffering may have vicarious value, somewhat like the prophets and Jesus. This is not to encourage indulgence in pathetic martyr thinking. Rather, it is a recognition that public experiences of pastors are often instructive for others.

Healing is the next major step toward recovery. Modern science teaches that the body, mind, and spirit have built-in interrelated healing processes that will produce basic healing if not interfered with. But sometimes outside toxic agents require more healing ability than the natural immune systems can provide. Therefore, medications and specialized care may be required.

Healing takes time. Pastors will need to devote adequate time to their part in the healing, such as extra rest, less stressful scheduling, healthier nutrition, and more positive diversions. Pastors also need to watch for relapses, especially if conflict and abuse continue. They must find special ways to protect themselves, or let others protect their wounds. If relapse occurs, the pastor must start over, assessing wounds, resources, and healing needs.

As healing begins, pastors need to make decisions about issues beyond immediate healing. Here is where coping strategies, resources, and career options need review. One of the looming decisions in serious conflict and abuse situations is whether or not to leave a congregation. Because it is natural for pastors to approach such decisions in a reactionary mode when they have been hurt, it is important to make use of a rational assessment process. Ten important factors need to be considered.

1. Personal fitness—How much more can I realistically handle without irreparable damage?
2. Effectiveness of church board and polity—Is there enough strength in the congregational system to manage this conflict effectively?
3. Support of denominational office—Can I depend on effective assistance from this source?
4. Operative support system—Does my support system have adequate resources available immediately?
5. Plan B (and C, D, E)—Are my alternatives adequate?
6. Effects on intimates—What will be best for my spouse, family, and other intimates?
7. Realistic severance package—How does the potential severance package influence this decision?
8. Effects on congregation—How would staying or leaving affect the congregation?
9. Legal considerations—How will this case sound in a court of law?
10. God's call—To what do I discern God is calling me? (This number one priority is last on this list because the other items must be

factored into our decision making as part of the way God leads us. If we begin by trying to assess God's calling for our decision, we are likely to idealize this call, or make the decision on the unrealistic basis of "oughts" and "shoulds.")

Your personal self-management, when under attack or traumatized, is a crucial issue. Self-management becomes difficult and complicated under heavy stress. Therefore, having a clear strategy, accepting assistance, and assessing realistic options require focused attention. Ideally, a pastor should have at least a tentative strategy for high-stress decisions before he or she needs it too desperately.

SKILLS FOR CONGREGATIONS

Even the finest pastor cannot save a congregation from the collateral damage that clergy killers produce when they go after an authority figure. Lay leaders such as church secretary, organist, custodian, or chairperson need to be aware that they may become targets of a clergy killer, for any leader a clergy killer perceives to be a rival or a barrier to their plans is likely to be targeted. Parishioners need to share responsibility for their own well-being and the wholeness of the congregation and its mission. This includes investing in, supporting, and protecting a primary congregational resource—its pastor.

Since institutionalized religion bought into the business model as its operational style, laity have been relegated to the role of spectators and stockholders. As spectators, they feel free to applaud or boo the performances of leaders. As stockholders, they feel free to criticize the CEO. It will take time for us to teach and learn the shared responsibilities of ministry in congregations again.

Congregations need to invest in and protect their pastor and other professional leaders; when its spiritual leaders are under attack, the ministries by and for parishioners suffer. Uninformed and theologically illiterate laity are vulnerable to the blandishments (threat, flattery, cajolery, and misrepresentation) of clergy killers.

Feedback I've received to my original column on clergy killers in *The Clergy Journal* (August 1993) indicates an obvious gap in church teaching materials. Many biblical and theological curricula are available, a few conflict management materials, but few resources that teach congregations about the realities of church politics, or the true nature of clergy killers and what to do about them. Until educational materials on this subject are commonly available, pastors must point out the key issues and be creative in their congregations. The basic ingredients are awareness, theological literacy, and conflict management.

It is apparent that most parishioners are unaware of church politics and feel little responsibility for them. Until they become aware of and can understand clergy killers, they will collude unintentionally with the destruction of clergy and congregations.

Theology can be a dry subject until lay people experience its value in explaining the Bible, evil, reconciliation, and ministries of ordinary believers. Without biblical and theological literacy, people are left to their own devices and vulnerabilities.

Finally, responsible parishioners need to learn about the realities of diversity, conflict, and abuse in congregational life. Clergy and laity together need to understand diversity and the normal conflicts this can generate, and how to negotiate differences through conflict management. It is important to understand the conflict potential in personality and mental disorders and to learn how to deal with evil in the form of demonic and cunning pseudo-believers. This requires enlightened skills in tough love strategies and interventions, discussed earlier.

Like skilled surgeons, the congregation must be prepared to excise the cancer that clergy killers induce. Even though denominational polities may provide only limited guidance for interventions, God's Holy Spirit, biblical insights, and contemporary clinical and legal knowledge can guide caring believers in the excision of clergy killers. Congregations can become so healthy that they are immunized to clergy killer infection.

One of the simplest and most specific ways to prevent escalation of conflict and development of clergy killers in a congregation is to develop and use a grievance procedure. Most denominational polities and congregational bylaws have at least a rudimentary method by which aggrieved parishioners may seek redress of real or imagined mistreatment or flaws in church activities. Often a serious conflict begins with a person who becomes frustrated at finding no one to listen to or remedy a complaint. It is surprising to find how few congregations have a clear, widely known procedure for handling complaints.

A complaint procedure should be based upon established polity and bylaws, of course, and it must be simple, effective, and known by parishioners. It usually consists of designating an officeholder to receive the complaint. The complaint is then brought to an official board or committee for review and recommendations. Then the elected officials of the congregation determine what shall be done with the complaint. Their decision is the final word, unless there is a legitimate higher judicatory with jurisdiction.

SKILLS FOR DENOMINATIONS

Though denominational officers are developing skills for dealing with conflict and abuse, the need for improvement in dealing with clergy killers is apparent. Denominational leaders need to give more attention to several matters:

First, they must develop awareness. When I consult with bishops and other leaders, I find that most are aware of local conflicts and some provide training in conflict management. But many do not understand the evil realities of clergy killers. Some even collude with clergy killers by pandering to their threats and presumed power. A few are clergy killers themselves, or at least they function this way for unfavored clergy under their care. Seminaries barely acknowledge conflict and clergy killers. So the first task for denominational personnel is the same as for clergy and parishioners: they need to see and believe the reality of clergy killers and evil in congregational life.

The second task, unique to denominational offices, is to develop political clout—policies and support necessary to undergird the good people and excise evil ones and their methods. Even in congregational styles of polity, denominational officials have a mystique that can tip the balance away from clergy killers in local struggles.

Handling clergy killers can be complicated for denominational leaders, since most bishops feel beholden to people they perceive to be powerbrokers in a congregation. If clergy killers are perceived as such, great courage is required to confront them. It is also apparent that standards for judging clergy and moving them are clearer than for judging and moving laity. We have now developed strong ethical codes for clergy. We will unbalance the system seriously if we do not do the same for laity.

Finally, denominational offices need to foster the research and development of clergy support systems. The breakdown and malfeasance statistics for clergy are high (upward of 25 percent) and rising. Because the health of the clergy is crucial to the health of the denomination, realistic clergy support is mandatory. This does not imply pampering incompetent and lazy clergy; it means encouraging all clergy toward excellence. It is obvious that traditional assumptions and strategies regarding clergy support are inadequate. Perhaps clergy, out of self-interest and pastoral concern for their families, and the church, can lead the way.

NOTES

12

BUILDING SUPPORT SYSTEMS

Support systems are more than a social and professional buzz word. They are vital to our personal wholeness and professional effectiveness. They are also dependable sources of healing, defense, guidance, and prevention of abuse.

As a profession, clergy need a clearer concept of support for their personal lives and ministry, and a model to serve as a guiding image. A tree, with its roots and the ecosystem that supports it, provides a relevant model; it is a living entity that produces benefits to many and yet it needs input to sustain its life and benefits. It is also interdependent with other living entities. Its primary resource is the energy of life. The tree is used specifically as the basis for an exercise that helps pastors evaluate their support system. (See Appendix A at the back of this book.)

BASIC PRINCIPLES

Though the support system concept seems familiar now to most people, familiarity does not mean pastors all understand or have built adequate support systems.

This is a brief primer on support systems—personal, professional, and organizational. We begin with the basic principles of support systems.

1. Everyone needs support systems.
2. Each person and group has support needs that are both similar and idiosyncratic.
3. Support systems are interdependent.
4. Support systems must adapt to change.
5. Support systems are about the management of energy.

Everyone needs support systems. Professional, health, and survival needs cannot be met in isolation. The illusions of "rugged individualism" do not fit contemporary opportunities and needs. In fact, we are born dependent and remain that way; we get sick when we forget what is required for health. The law of consequences says that all behavior has consequences. These consequences are good or bad, depending on how they meet human needs and the needs of creation, and whether they meet the criteria of our beliefs and traditions.

The needs of each person and group are both similar and idiosyncratic. Individuals are unique in some ways and similar in others. This uniqueness and similarity factor pertains to all of creation. Like the great watering holes of Africa where a variety of animals share the water but drink in different ways, so our ecosystem nurtures our common needs and accepts differences. While human beings have similar needs, each must adapt to the available ecosystem. This is the principle of individuation by which ecosystems encourage uniqueness within systems.

Support systems are interdependent. We are learning about the law of interdependency in which all functioning systems (material, economic, ecological, political, moral, and so forth) interact and are interdependent. We now breathe each other's pollutants, drink each other's liquids, eat each other's products, and pay each other's bills. Even our religions are now interrelated through ecumenism, media coverage, international politics, and such. When we pervert our sharing, all suffer eventually. When we cooperate, the synergy that results can benefit many.

Support systems must adapt to change. Contemporary change is enigmatic. On one hand we must adapt or die. On the other hand, "the more things change, the more they stay the same." Human experience throughout history indicates that basic human needs—survival, self-expression, relationships, and morality—remain constant, while the expression of them varies.

The law of basics indicates that when any of these needs is not met adequately, or is overindulged in relationship to the others, some kind of sickness unto death results.

Support systems are about the management of energy. The whole of God's creation is dynamic, meaning it is constantly in motion. This motion is a function of energy, which is the stuff of life. Any action uses and distributes energy, says the law of dynamism. For us as human beings, it is a reminder that we are not the source of energy and life. God is. We only receive, use, and distribute energy. Therefore, if we are to avoid burnout (the loss of ability to use energy), we must manage the energy available to us according to a basic principle of energy management which says that energy taken in must equal energy given out.

UNDERSTANDING PERSONAL ENERGY

Many people do not understand personal energy, thus are poorly equipped to manage it. We must begin by becoming aware of physical, mental, emotional, and spiritual forms of energy. And we must begin to note how our handling of these forms of energy affects our lives and ministries.

The principle of transformation is an enormously hopeful and challenging reality. Because transformation is occurring continually in the physical, mental, and spiritual realm, we may participate in it by learning how it works. Not only does energy ebb and flow and vitalize our lives, it provides infinite possibilities for creative change, for good or evil, even as sunlight can both nurture and burn. God the Creator has modeled the creative potential by turning chaos into a "good" creation. God the Redeemer demonstrated the ability to transmute evil into good, death into eternal life. And God the Sustainer continually offers the miracles of healing, renewal, and transformation in everyday living. Therefore, a worthy support system not only sustains life, it can be the womb of transformation.

THE INGREDIENTS OF SUPPORT

As mentioned earlier, the basic metaphor or analogy used for a support system here is a tree. Though not a perfect model, it leads us to useful insights. It has a trunk, branches, leaves, fruit, roots, and it exists in an interactive environment. (Jesus' use of the vine as metaphor in John 15 is enlightening, as is Psalm 1 in the Older Testament.) Trees are an expression of creativity and energy. The management of trees is a continuous discipline.

Each support system must provide nurture for that which it is intended to support. The following version of such a system is intended to support pastors of local congregations. The acronym S-U-P-P-O-R-T may be helpful:

S—Services. This is the mix of ingredients necessary for healthy personal and professional living. From food production to waste management, from secretarial services to placement services, we need assistance from others for survival, personally and professionally. A functional support system locates and contracts for such services.

U—Undergirding. Although we try to focus our lives and ministry on spiritual issues, we become aware that money is significant in our society. Without adequate amounts of it, our lives and ministries are limited. Therefore, our support system requires access to this facilitator in sufficient amounts for healthy and effective ministry.

P—Political advocacy. Because we are social beings and our actions are interdependent, we need each other. This interaction includes politics (how people organize their interaction) and the possibility of inadvertent and intentional harm from people within the immediate system. Unless I (or my systems) wish to spend much time defending myself, my congregation and denomination must help make the political systems in which I function as safe as possible. Moreover, the congregation and denomination must help make it safe for me to take the risk of responsible, prophetic ministry. I, of course, still retain primary responsibility for my own safety and actions.

P—Protocol. Spiritual leadership is undergoing significant change. A variety of leaders purporting to point out spiritual truth, and the rise of secularism are eroding the traditional authority of clergy. Without trust and respect, clergy cannot function effectively. Therefore, pastors and lay spiritual leaders must share responsibility for ensuring that denominational polity and congregational bylaws are upgraded and practiced for guidance and protection of pastors and their intimates.

O—Opportunity. One basic human need is to experience personal and shared achievement. Without sense of achievement, a person does not appreciate and fully understand herself or himself. A support system must not only allow opportunity for personal and shared achievement, it must help facilitate it. Without this, the spiritual gifts and graces that nurture the faith community are stunted.

R—Relationships. Few factors are as important to a support system as the network of people with whom we form intimate, fraternal, and professional relationships. Each person's social needs are unique. But everyone needs at least one intimate partner, one close friend, and one dependable professional colleague. And there must be someone available to answer 911 calls in emergencies. Such relationships work best when they are two-way. In spiritual leadership the key words are relationship, relationship, and relationship—healthy relationships within myself, with God, and with others.

T—Training. Both human society and the roles that facilitate are in transition. While some traditional practices are retained in contemporary vocations, adaptations and growth are required for the changes that are occurring. Therefore, interactive opportunities for growth and evaluation of functioning are not optional. Change and growth are crucial to wholeness—of people and of systems. Therefore, support must include this element.

Appendix B, "Supportive Relationship Inventory," offers an opportunity to assess your professional support system. To use it, you can put a check mark in the Now or the Needed column to indicate the status of this item for you. When you have finished, this inventory can serve as a prescription for healthier professional functioning.

THE PASTOR NEEDS A PASTOR

These same ingredients just discussed are necessary for individual support. But they are required as well for personal and institutional and support systems. Marriages and families need them. Congregations need them. Denominations need them. Each social clustering needs these ingredients in ways that nurture its unique needs. And each shares the responsibility for building and maintaining its support system.

A congregational-denominational support process must be based upon this individual model if it is to be effective. Our emphasis here, however, is on the individual pastor's personal and professional support systems.

Among clergy, the primary adaptation required for combining the ingredients mentioned above into a realistic support system may be termed "Being your own pastor." This is the missing ingredient in many pastors' (and partners' and families') lives. The oft-repeated truism, "The pastor of the church is the only member who has no pastor," is ominous, for if we presume that any normal human being needs a pastor, it follows that pastors are either superhuman or nonhuman. Because neither is likely, we must assume that either our presumptions are wrong, or that many pastors suffer from lack of pastoring. The latter is true in my experience.

It is important to note that being my own pastor means accepting primary responsibility for seeing that I receive adequate pastoring. It does not mean that I can do all this pastoring for myself. The being-your-own-pastor issue also raises an implied condemnation—that denominational officials designated as "pastor to pastors" are not doing the job. Experienced pastors know that, in reality, denominational officials are typically expected to fulfill two functions: administration and pastoring. But these typically are at odds with each other. If administration is primary in the denominational office, the interests of pastors will be secondary, except as pastors benefit from maintenance of the bureaucracy. If pastoring is primary, it is likely that the pastoring will be applied more readily to congregants than to pastors, for congregants contribute to budgets and are not under established rules of discipline. Pastors seeing this tend not to trust efforts at pastoring them. Therefore, though denominational leaders often intend to pastor pastors (and their families), the political realities limit this intention.

When pastors try to function as their own pastors, or even as pastors to family and friends, they experience professional limitations similar to those that affect physicians, lawyers, and other human service professionals. Pastors typically have other roles—spouse, parent, friend—that preempt the pastoral role. Or the pastor might not be accepted as pastor by these family members and friends. These realities help explain some of the illusions and failures when a pastor is trying to be a pastor to family, friends—and self.

The pastor who believes she can be her own pastor is a naive pastor. Most of the distortions in the thinking of parishioners are also present in pastors. Pastors are capable of self-deception as well, for they may imagine their self-pastoring is more effective than it is, or that by doing the same things for themselves as they do for parishioners, the need is met. Pastors may also do the pastoring perfunctorily, with the hidden assumption that such pastoring is not really needed. (After all, aren't pastors ordained, and didn't they graduate from seminary, and didn't God's "call" provide them with immunity from human needs?)

Because a pastor is so intimately involved in providing pastoral services to others, it may seem awkward to suggest that the pastor provide these services for himself. This discomfort may cause a pastor to go through a kind of pastoral checklist perfunctorily, in which case the outcome of the pastoring is likely to be indifferent also. And yet such a checklist (see the traditional pattern below) is important in order that a pastor see what is missing.

A more serious danger in self-pastoring, however, is the numbness and boredom of overfamiliarity in that a pastor thinks she knows herself better than she does. She may also be tired of administering pastoral care today and ignore her own needs. Pastors do not intend this and are often unaware of such reactions to the pastoral process. But this is a normal, predictable response to repetition, even in activities and professions in which dedication and inspiration are expected to be prominent motivators.

A pastor who is serious about evaluating personal pastoral needs might begin by reviewing the "services" people traditionally expect to receive:

1. Personal contacts, a "pastoral presence"
2. Admonition and encouragement
3. Officiating at significant events
4. Sermons and teaching
5. Sickness or crisis ministrations
6. Encouragement of mission and stewardship
7. Leadership in worship and spiritual disciplines

Personal contact with a "pastoral presence" describes the myriad informal contacts a pastor makes because he is a pastor, and that usually bring emotional and spiritual benefit. It is not likely that a pastor can do this adequately. However, a pastor can benefit from journaling, talking thoughtfully to himself while looking in a mirror, by taping conversations to himself, and so on. These suggestions might sound uncomfortable to do, but they can be therapeutic with a little practice.

Admonition and encouragement—advice, directives, and affirmation— are needed by pastors. When sin is present, it is named. When confusion is present, spiritual guidelines are offered. When there is positive achievement, growth, and mission, these are reinforced with recognition. Pastors can do this ministry for themselves, but this requires honesty and spiritual discipline.

The actions are more likely to have the needed impact if another spiritual leader provides the care.

Officiating at significant events is an unlikely ingredient in self-pastoring; part of the value in such officiating lies in the officiant being an outsider, a representative of the church and of God who recognizes the event. A common complaint of pastors is that no church official recognized some special event in their lives. Because this is an important function, pastors should consider helping peers become aware of the significant event and request some response, or else simply settle for celebrating it themselves. This is the same bind some parishioners are in when they want the pastor to read their mind and honor their event without sharing responsibility for informing him of the event and their feelings.

Preaching and teaching are functions pastors often do for themselves subconsciously, for it is an open secret that many sermons and class lessons are self-serving, in good and bad ways. Pastors, however, do need to hear sermons and good instruction as models for their own ministry. They also need to sit under good preaching and teaching for their own spiritual health. This they cannot do for themselves. Peers and colleagues must fill the gap.

Ministrations to pain, crisis, and grief are also difficult to administer to oneself, since much of the value derives from an outsider's caring and ministering grace to the need. It means a lot to have a pastor minister to you in these circumstances, especially if it is one whom you know and respect. If it isn't going to happen unless you request it from another pastor, then request it. I know from experience that this can work well.

The encouragement of mission and stewardship seems redundant, as many pastors meet or exceed lay standards in these areas. However, pastors should realize that lay people are expected to volunteer over and above the time spent in their vocation. By this standard, clergy should be available after regular pastoring hours for typical volunteer tasks like anyone else. Some pastors need to push themselves on this one, for it can be highly motivating for parishioners to see the pastor volunteering beside them. Others need to free themselves from unrealistic expectations in this regard.

Worship, especially spiritual disciplines, is not standard practice for many Protestant clergy. Catholic and high church clergy are usually expected to lead themselves or others through liturgy and spiritual disciplines daily (see the Spiritual Disciplines Pyramid in Chapter 13), or even more often. Many evangelical, conservative, and liberal pastors are also well disciplined, though less liturgical. For Protestant clergy, the pattern ranges from no personal participation beyond that done in preparation and leadership of worship for others, to following highly disciplined spiritual regimens each day. This is a function pastors can and must do for themselves if they wish to maintain spiritual viability. It also helps to do at least some of these disciplines with ordained colleagues. Spiritual kinship among spiritual leaders is a nurturing experience.

FINDING A PASTOR

If pastors are willing to be responsible for their own pastoring, then they must be willing to reach out to our clergy peers for the pastoring they cannot do for themselves. Even when pastors use all their best pastoring skills and methods on themselves, there will be missing ingredients. Pastors who are honest with themselves about self-pastor responsibilities will accept or call for pastoring from others. (We should note that there are gender, ethnic, sexual orientation, and age variations in the needs of pastors. These must be factored into individual support systems, lest some nurturing factor be missing.)

In some pastoral functions, lay people can minister effectively to pastors, if both accept such ministrations and they are done competently and ethically. Pastoral ministry is a two-way process—giving and receiving. Parishioners pray for, support, encourage, provide hospitality, admonish, preach, and on occasion administer sacraments to pastors. But pastors and laity need to be reminded of this two-way process; the natural tendency is to be distracted by role disparities and varying skill levels.

There is a great deal of concern recently for observing "boundaries" in pastoral ministry. This is an important issue because some pastors have forgotten how to keep themselves under professional discipline as they minister. Some have never learned the value of keeping professional discipline between themselves and parishioners. A number of church leaders, however, believe that ministry from ordained clergy is better than that of lay people; that pastors must be aloof from laity; and that professional rules should take the place of common sense and caring. I am most certainly not advocating or defending irresponsibility and license, and I have warned against these. But I offer a reminder that pastoral ministry is an art—a spiritual art. It must be driven by vision and discernment. When it is confined by inappropriate rules, its soul is diminished. The church is presently in a valuable period of reviewing boundaries and rules. Although there is need for more dialogue before rules are hardened, when a pastor has any questions about whether an action is appropriate, the pastor should take the most cautious approach.

A healthy, competent, and spiritually disciplined pastor must have some freedom to minister on the basis of pastoral wisdom, as well as professional boundaries and rules. Pastors must, of course, keep reminding each other to recognize professional boundaries; they avoid many vulnerabilities and problems by understanding limits—their own and those of others. The key factor here is the same as it has always been: recognizing the needs of the parishioner as a guide to professional ministrations. This means seeing past the presenting problem and the titillating possibilities to the need for spiritual healing and health. A corollary factor here is that when a pastor feels doubt about a pastoral situation, she should not act precipitously and should withdraw for prayer and thought before acting. One of the best safeguards against boundary violations is to think through all ministry situations before they happen, if at all possible.

It is very important for pastors to recognize that they cannot fully pastor themselves. A variety of helpful resources are available. Pastoral counselors can advise and counsel in issues of mental health and faith. Spiritual directors (sometimes called by other names) may be available to assist in spiritual formation and growth. Catholic priests are required to have a personal confessor or spiritual director. Many Protestant pastors are finding such a person invaluable. Mentors are colleagues or peers who offer guidance and support as a pastor to the pastor, or some specialty significant to pastoring. More pastors and denominations are realizing the value of counselors, spiritual directors, or mentors to offset the vulnerabilities resulting from lonerism in pastoral ministry.

PEER KEEPER GROUPS

"Peer keeper groups" is the name I give to a model of clergy support groups. These groups can take a variety of forms (lectionary study, athletic, hobby), but the intent is always to encourage growth and caring among pastors. These groups seem to be most effective when kept small (six to ten members). Larger groups are possible, of course, but if larger they should include regular breakout activities in which smaller groupings promote more intimate interaction. My research also shows that the leaderless group model is one of the most useful for peer keeper groups. This helps to avoid the complications of hierarchical models. In this model, leadership is by consensus with temporary leaders selected for specific purposes, such as serving as convener for a meeting or series of events. The informality of leaderless groups can produce pitfalls, such as lack of purpose, confusing agendas, and lack of accountability. The group must take responsibility for the shared purpose, which in general is to affirm and care for each other, and more specifically to accomplish consensual goals.

The core of a peer keeper group is its trust covenant. This covenant can contain anything the group decides together. Here are four ingredients that I find important:

1. Each person is responsible for his or her own needs and for communicating them if assistance is desired.

2. No one needs to prove anything to the group. No performances are required. Each person can be himself or herself, as long as he or she is willing to live with the consequences of his or her behavior.

3. No participant may tell another participant's "story" (whatever is shared of a personal nature) outside the group. When participants share information about themselves, this remains his or her own personal property and is confidential to the group unless otherwise instructed by the teller. Each member is free to tell his or her own story, of course, but always with sensitivity to each other's needs. If this confidentiality is violated, whether known to the teller or not, the group should see that the steps of confession, forgiveness, penance, and absolution are followed.

4. The group holds each participant accountable for personal and professional conduct, not necessarily with rules, but with consensual standards, caring, and disciplines.

PROFESSIONAL ORGANIZATIONS AND NETWORKS

Professional organizations for clergy have a mixed history. It is notoriously difficult to keep clergy organized unless the benefits and costs are clear and strong. But one that deserves mention is the Academy of Parish Clergy. Its emphasis is on collegiality, competence, ethical accountability, and continuing education. Members are urged to select one of four "pathways" of professional growth, which is reviewed and celebrated by peers. It also features special awards for excellence and extraordinary achievements. It is organized into regional chapters and publishes a quarterly journal. (Write to Academy of Parish Clergy, 13500 Shaker Blvd., Suite 601, Cleveland, OH 44120.)

"Network" is the term usually used for the informal and personal supporters a pastor selects over a period of time to be supportive in particular ways. This network may consist of special friends, professional specialists, confidants, mentors, therapists, spiritual directors, and even fantasy people (a remembered and revered person, a storybook character, an "angel," an alter ego, and so on). It is easier now to communicate with and make use of a network of specialists through vehicles such as E-mail, Fax, Internet, and telephone. Networking is an important ingredient in any clergy person's support system. Without an active, diverse, dependable network, a pastor easily becomes a loner and misses a significant amount of the nurture, guidance, and accountability necessary for fitness in pastoral ministry.

Along with these individual supporters, there are collegial groups within denominations that, though they may seem unnecessary to some, can be supportive for many clergy. Continuing education opportunities stimulate, inspire, and provide networking opportunities. Career evaluation centers provide serious clinical evaluations and career strategies for times of crisis and transitions, or for regular checkups.

In 1995 I surveyed Minnesota clergy for the Minnesota Council of Churches regarding how clergy experienced their support systems. These are some of my findings:

>+ Two-thirds indicated pervasive stress.
>+ "Lack of adequate time" was the biggest problem.
>+ The most important support factor was spouse and family.
>+ More than half who participated are in peer support groups.
>+ Eighty percent want pastoral counseling available.

Compared to classic studies of pastors a generation ago, these data are quite similar. Noticeable change is present, however, in the percentage of pastors participating in support groups, and the percentage wanting to have pastoral counseling available for themselves and their intimates. (See Edgar W.

Mills and John P. Koval, *Stress in Ministry* [Washington D.C.: Ministry Studies Board, 1971] and Gerald J. Jud, et al., *Ex-Pastors* [Philadelphia: Pilgrim Press, 1970].)

Support resources are valuable for nurturing health, the prevention of clergy breakdowns, and for crisis management. The maintenance of wholeness, wellness, and fitness is a better goal than disaster relief, because good health, when it becomes a habit, can be sustained even under crisis and high stress.

PSEUDOSUPPORT

It is important to remind ourselves that there are forms of clergy support which produce support that is neither sound nor genuine. We all have probably encountered this type of "support," but it is not always easy to spot. This is another reason for periodic review of support systems. Please be aware that what follows is only a partial list of pseudosupport types, and that some of the forms of support listed may also be helpful and supportive in realistic ways if managed and used better.

At the congregational level are the traditional and notorious "palace guards," the sycophants and cohorts whom pastors may gather around themselves to reinforce a fragile ego, do their bidding, act as informers, and act as shills for favored projects. There are usually naive parishioners willing to serve in this coterie, if a pastor is guileful enough to encourage them in such roles.

Then there are members who pretend to be supportive but are not, for their own devious or subconscious reasons. A few members who are mentally or personality disordered may try to attach themselves to a pastor. Such a pastor is responsible to treat such people sensitively, and to work to get them the needed therapy or support. Others may intend to be sincerely supportive but are actually unreliable, for whatever reasons, when there is controversy. It is a rule of thumb that if a pastor allows a member to get into a position of having to choose between loyalty to the pastor and loyalty to another parishioner (particularly a powerbroker), the pastor will lose this support.

More serious and subtle is the pseudosupport of codependents. Codependence is a term from modern psychology that refers to two or more persons who bond with each other around detrimental and subconscious agendas. The original designation referred to people who collude in substance abuse, who keep this abuse secret, and who protect those who indulge their habit safe from consequences. The meaning has been broadened in popular usage to mean people who collude in behavior that damages innocent parties, sabotages legitimate programs, or eventually harms the codependents themselves. A congregational conspiracy is the most notorious version of codependency. Here two or more members decide to sabotage a church program or harm a member for their own benefit. It is more common for people to form cliques, promote deleterious agendas, and relate to each other in harmful ways, any of which may appear to be innocent or harmless.

The solution to codependence is not to become isolated from others. Healthy marriages, working relationships, or temporary alliances, for example, require that the parties to some degree be *interdependent*. The key to the negativity of codependencies is their resistance to reality and openness, and the likelihood of long-term harm that will override potential benefits. In positive relationships, each party derives real and healthy benefits—a symbiotic relationship. As long as the healthy benefits outweigh the negative costs, this is useful. It takes courage to see and act to end codependencies. But wise pastors learn how to differentiate codependencies from interdependencies, how to avoid codependencies, and even to help break them up where damage is predictable. It also takes courage to recognize the temptation to depreciate some useful relationships simply because they are not perfect.

Along with these negative systems and their obvious remedies, we must note the need for a realistic process to assess congregations and help pastors identify destructive systems. As mentioned earlier, we now have effective methods for assessing how pastors relate to their congregations and for disciplining malefactors, but very few effective ways to assess how congregations treat their pastors. This is not only patently unfair, but it is also costing the church enormous amounts of money and energy in hidden and obvious ways. The informal word-of-mouth method by which some pastors tell others the truth about congregations they have pastored is not reliable nor widespread enough. Denominational offices must realize this need and develop such a system, or pastors will have to develop their networking more effectively.

As indicated earlier, it is beyond the purview of this book to advise denominational offices on strategies and remedies for the conflict and abuse in their congregations. However, based upon research and anecdotal experience, we must note the negative support factors common to some officials. First is the "fire the manager" attitude in which officials find it easier to move a pastor than deal with trouble in the congregation. In fairness we must recognize that denominational politics and lack of resources make it difficult for officials to support some pastors or investigate problem congregations. But we must also recognize that this attitude is unfair to many pastors and detrimental to the denominations in the long term.

The call system of a denomination can also be a source of pseudosupport and is a convenient way to punish or act out prejudices. The people-pleasing bishop is likewise often a source of pseudosupport, for that untrustworthy smile and quick reassurance may not represent true support in time of trouble. Some officials have come to believe it is more important to pacify a congregation than support the office of pastor. Some pastors, on the other hand, have unrealistic expectations of denominational officials and are unwilling to be supportive of those they don't like. This pseudosupport can work both ways.

Seminaries, professors, and the academic model also sometimes provide pseudosupport for local church pastors, in general and when under attack. Seminary professors, for example, are least likely to be consulted in the list of resource persons troubled pastors may turn to for support. The academic model that is standard for training in seminaries is showing inadequate adaptability to the real needs of contemporary pastoring, particularly for dealing with conflict and abuse. Some professors are developing conflict resolution methods, but they tend to be too complicated or idealistic for dealing with the realities of human behavior on the congregational level.

It should be obvious that all of us need more and different kinds of support than the traditional model of pastoring indicated. Pastors do not need support because they are weak, but because they are human and are called to a complicated and draining role. We must remind ourselves that though the new and old needs of pastors are becoming more obvious, it remains up to each of us, and all of us together, to build the necessary support for healthful living and effective ministry.

The appendixes provide two aids for evaluating a support system. Appendix A, "Supportive Relationship Inventory," and Appendix B, "Energy Management Inventory," address the issue of wholeness from different perspectives.

13

PASTORAL FITNESS

A fresh metaphor for self-care and competence in ministry is "fitness." The benefits of fitness are enormous. It deserves a place in our consideration of conflict resolution, healing, self-care, and self-management. If we are to handle our wounds, our failures, and our stewardship, we need to have a clear picture in our minds of what health and fitness are.

In the previous chapter, we discussed support systems. Here we will discuss self-management—for pastors who are wounded and under attack, and in normal pastoring. In the last chapter we will expand this concept of fitness to the whole community of faith in a discussion of healthy congregations.

Fitness has much in common with other terms we have considered, such as health, wholeness, wellness, and competence, but it has a specific meaning that is pertinent to self-care and ministry. As used here, fitness means conditioning body, mind, and spirit to fulfill God's purposes.

The term "fitness" has become part of the physical awareness culture in our society. In such usage it tends to refer to strength, flexibility, aerobic capacity, and coordination.

For our purposes, such understandings may be helpful, but they can also be misleading. Fitness for ministry is not about muscles, appearances, or heroic performances, though these have some value as analogies. Pastoral fitness means organic health, professional competence, and spiritual discipline.

When we are young we tend to imagine that health comes naturally, and it often does. As we mature, however, the consequences of our self-care and the effects of genes and environment begin to show. We must then spend time compensating for past mistakes and influences and learn to develop healthy self-management regimens while recognizing our limitations and assets.

Busyness, both real and imagined, has become an enormous mental block—an attitude—in our society. When we perceive ourselves as very busy, we have a built-in excuse to force ourselves into stressful schedules and expectations. This then allows us to rationalize overindulgence in coping mechanisms such as eating for entertainment, sleeping for comfort, using chemical substances for relaxation, and postponing good self-care. Recent research has shown that we are becoming less physically fit, in spite of the fitness fads and warnings about flabbiness. We use television, computer games, and vacuous activities as stress reducers, in spite of warnings about mental laziness. Busyness also becomes an excuse for spiritual bulimia in which we gorge on spiritual junk food, then must purge to start over.

Such attitudes have obviously infected the spiritual community. It is harder to find volunteers for church work; many claim busyness as an excuse, though many are sincerely too busy due to economic needs. Leaders do not do their homework or accept training. And pastors have less time for spiritual disciplines.

No, this is not a call for guilt trips. It is a wakeup call for those of us who have accepted the privilege of spiritual leadership. It is a simple fact that fitness leads to competence and responsible stewardship of talents and leadership commitments. Fitness is also a fine resource or condition for coping with conflict, clergy killer attacks, and other tough issues in ministry. When we are physically fit we experience less pain, we are less vulnerable, and we have more endurance and more flexibility. Experience indicates this is true also for mental and spiritual fitness. It follows then that if we keep ourselves fit for ministry, we not only suffer less, we also model health for the church.

Aunt Collie, a wise lay leader I once encountered in a backwoods church, is still a guiding memory for me as a person who offered pearls of wisdom. I remember two of her aphorisms that pertain to the plagues of busyness and flabbiness.

First, "There's always enough time." I heard her make this remark to parishioners who were worried about getting the church building ready for a meeting on time. When she said, "There's always enough time," she was not being irresponsible. She was reminding them that when our priorities are right, the important things get done. Arranging the chairs for the meeting was not as important as having a meeting where people really meet, and where spiritual needs are met. She was reminding all of us that we only have so much time to work with. Therefore, relaxing into our ministry priorities allows mission to happen, whether the expectations that lead to busyness are met or not. And the energy toll is much smaller.

Second, "We get sick when we forget how to be well." In saying this, Aunt Collie reminds us that if we get sick or dysfunctional, we will be forced to take time to take care of ourselves and to set aside other responsibilities. It makes more sense to keep ourselves healthy. When we occasionally become ill, if we are basically fit we are likely to recover more quickly and have fewer long-term consequences.

Healing is an important part of fitness. Healing comes before fitness. And healing is enhanced by fitness. When we are wounded and exhausted, we tend to look for magical answers to our discomfort. Healing will occur if we allow it to happen, for God has built this potential into us. But healing requires us to manage our time and energy less stressfully. When healing is complete, we can concentrate on fitness. This may be a good time to review the discussion of recovery and healing in Chapter 3 on collateral damage.

FITNESS AS A WAY OF LIFE

My experience indicates that pastors do not typically spend enough time on bodily fitness. This is one of the reasons why clergy, who once topped the actuarial tables at insurance companies, have deteriorated to a point where our health resembles national averages. Because pastoring has become a high-stress profession, we can expect our unfit bodies, minds, and spirits to succumb to the maladies of stress we see all around us—unless we make better use of the fitness metaphor. More specifically, pastors under attack or in conflict typically cease wise management of their bodies and use their appetites as stress reducers. (I recently prepared a booklet on fitness for pastors, *Fit to Be a Pastor*. It is now offered by the National Association of

Religious Professionals to encourage wellness among clergy. It may be ordered from NARP at 400 Robert Street North, St. Paul, MN 55101-2098, or phone 1-800-924-6277.)

Fitness is a subheading under wholeness, which is the union of body, mind, and spirit in the fulfillment of God's purposes. But wholeness is becoming a cliche in our society, and it is not a precise enough term to guide our thinking and motivate behavior. For a helpful book on this subject, consider Howard Clinebell's *Well Being* (San Francisco: Harper San Francisco, 1992). This excellent resource book discusses and illustrates seven aspects of well-being including physical, mental, and spiritual wholeness. Dr. Don Franks, author of *Fitness Facts, The Healthy Living Handbook* (Champaign: Human Kinetics Books, 1989, p. 3), says, "Total fitness is multidimensional—it is difficult to imagine the highest quality of life without including intellectual, social, spiritual and physical components. These aspects of life are interrelated in that a high level of fitness in one area enhances all other areas, and conversely a low fitness level in any area restricts the accomplishments possible in other areas."

FITNESS FOR THE BODY

Fitness requires continuing education for the body, because physical fitness doesn't just happen. Even when fitness is achieved, it erodes without an enlightened regimen of conditioning. This might already be intimidating for those who are unfit and find it difficult to accept the prospect of disciplined fitness. So, let me share some simple reminders that I use on myself when I feel resistance to my fitness regimen:

» It is less difficult to maintain fitness than to cope with the consequences of "unfitness" (sluggishness, illness, disrespect, poor self-image and low self-confidence).

» Fitness produces a "celebration" of good feelings, increased energy, and improved appearance.

» I can vary my fitness routines and even make them playful and fun when I am bored.

» My stewardship of body, mind, and spirit requires fitness—short-term and long-term. Fitness equals positive consequences, celebration, fun, and stewardship.

In his classic book *Embodiment* (Minneapolis: Augsburg Publishing House, 1978, Chapter 2), James B. Nelson reminds us that the way we think and feel about ourselves as bodies influences the way we think and feel about the world and about God. We deceive ourselves if we imagine we can be fully effective in pastoral ministry if we do not keep our bodies fit.

We always need to remind ourselves, of course, that physical fitness is not about beauty, strength, and heroics. It is about keeping our bodies as well conditioned for life and ministry as they can be. Few people have perfect bodies, and many must live with limitations and extraordinary physical challenges, but everyone can enjoy fitness, because fitness is not a matter of physical perfection and hubris. It is essentially a matter of stewardship.

It may be useful to remind ourselves of the basic process that leads to fitness for body, mind, and spirit. First we set a goal (mental image, vision), then make a decision (covenant), develop a plan (commitment), and manage ourselves (discipline). Finally, we enjoy healthy functioning (ministry, relationships, accomplishments). These are the ingredients of a continuing education course in physical fitness, with an emphasis on both "continuing" and "education." If you can't find such a course, you can do it yourself. Most of us have found that achieving physical fitness comes down to simply doing it, and then enjoying the benefits.

The image can begin with a full-length mirror or photo of yourself. That's right—be honest about your body, one of God's gifts to you, which you are responsible to manage well. Viewing this real picture means coming to terms with our physical selves—not perfect, not bad, but our visible selves.

Now, I need a realistic mental picture of me moving toward the bodily fitness that is realistic for me. This may require an investment: a consultation with a physical therapist, a certified aerobics or exercise instructor, and a physician who knows your body well.

If you are working toward fitness, you may find it supportive to make a covenant with yourself (and perhaps God and some trusted friends) to move toward fitness. You will need to reinforce this covenant again and again, as you vote by your actions to improve your stewardship of your body. Such actions develop a satisfying relationship between you, God, and others, which can help you absorb setbacks and support recovery efforts.

By the time you are solidifying your commitment to a way of life that includes wise care of your body, you can feel the difference. Even if you were in pretty good shape before, consistent movement toward greater fitness feels good. The discipline comes in simply doing the regimen you have chosen, whether you feel like it or not. You don't waste time and energy arguing with yourself. You just go ahead and do what you need to do.

Soon you notice a positive difference in energy, attitude, and feedback from others. This is when your regimen becomes a habit, which no longer requires planning and struggle. You follow your regimen and turn more thought and energy toward doing and enjoying the things that make life worthwhile—healthy functioning, healthy relationships, healthy ministries.

There are four tools for achieving physical fitness: exercise, nutrition, rest, and self-management. Your continuing education course has taught you the exercise part, so we move on to nutrition. The basics are food, water, and oxygen.

NUTRITION

The US Department of Agriculture provides us with recommendations about nutrition from the former Surgeon General, C. Everett Koop, in the Food Guide Pyramid. This is reliable instruction on nutrition which we ignore at our peril. Not only do we learn what foods to eat, we begin to learn how little we really need to sustain fitness, which can lead to eating less. Then we begin to understand the stewardship of food resources. There is plenty for all, if each of us settles for just enough. We can find joy (instead of pleasure) in eating less and feeling better.

Nutrition includes hydration—the intake of healthful fluids. We are learning surprising information about hydration. Most of us need more fluid than we take in, for thirst is not a reliable guide. The rule of thumb is six to eight eight-ounce glasses of water per day, besides what is contained in our food. This is one of the simplest and most beneficial changes most of us can make in our lives; it enhances alertness, empowers the immune system, and raises energy levels.

Oxygenation is also part of nature, so breathing correctly—and breathing clean air—contributes toward fitness. A continuing education course in correct breathing can aid digestion, relieve stress, clear the mind, and promote creativity. Fitness needs oxygen, but physically fit people also use oxygen more efficiently.

REST

Rest is a part of fitness we seldom consider realistically. It is important because it is nature's healing and recovery time. Sleep research indicates six to seven hours of sleep a night is appropriate for most situations and life stages. As we achieve and maintain fitness, this will feel adequate. Pacing ourselves with relaxation times, naps, and varying our activities is part of rest management.

SELF-MANAGEMENT

The self-management part of physical fitness includes addressing all of the above issues. It also includes developing an understanding of our chronobiology. This is the combination of cycles, rhythms, and biochemical reactions continually occurring in our bodies. "Our bodies don't lie" has been the slogan of specialists who are helping us understand the importance of learning the body's rhythms and moving *with* them, instead of ignoring or overriding them. For example, doing our strenuous work during our higher energy times of day usually lessens fatigue.

Perhaps it is useful to recognize again that writing on a subject like fitness can begin to sound preachy, and may only trigger guilt trips or resentment. I intend something different—to give strong encouragement for fitness. There is a growing realization that we who "talk the talk must walk the walk" in order to be believable. We may resent this modeling function in the clergy role. But it is a great opportunity to demonstrate the biblical ideal of wholeness, which includes struggles and failures as well as achievements. Wholeness is work worthy of our effort. It opens us all to God's grace, and is the core of pastoral ministry.

FITNESS FOR THE MIND

Fitness requires continuing education for the mind. Mental fitness doesn't just happen, and having a graduate degree does not ensure wisdom. Indeed, degrees may camouflage the absence of wisdom.

Thinking—good thinking, that is—is a crucial function of leadership. Leadership in this era of massive change and confusion requires mental skills beyond normal thought. A spiritual leader today must be able to distinguish what is helpful from our tradition, be creative in the society's ferment, and be able to discern God's purposes for the future. These can be accomplished by pastors with mental fitness. (See my column, "Thinking: the Principle Task of Leaders," in *The Clergy Journal*, October 1993.)

Our continuing education strategy should include course work and readings in creativity. It should include experiential and supervised work in disciplined thinking. It should include the development of spiritual discernment. And it should include information on how the human brain functions, how to nourish it, and how to relax it.

Just as with physical fitness, there is a basic process for achieving mental fitness. First we develop a goal, the mental image or "vision" we have of our minds functioning at their best. It may have been a long time since you tried to generate a picture of your brain functioning well, unencumbered by distress, and free of the numbing effects of fatigue, poor nutrition, or substance abuse. But this is worth some effort, for improving fitness begins with a clear, realistic picture of our current personal fitness.

After (sometimes before) we form the image, we need to initiate a strategy of mental fitness. Then comes the commitment to develop and sustain such fitness; often, the discipline of maintaining and growing mental skills becomes a pleasant habit (we insist on thinking healthy, positive, realistic thoughts and give less mental energy to "junk food"). The natural results of such fitness are increased mental alertness and energy, healthier relationships, and more thoughtful ministry.

MENTAL EXERCISES

How is mental fitness achieved? The basic tools are similar to physical fitness. Mental exercises are one tool. Our brains love to think. In fact, they do this constantly, whether we are aware of it or not. Our only choice is how we manage this process. It is likely that each of us must learn how to exercise our brains systematically, since few of us are taught the skills of mental exercise and development. Following is a brief discussion of several mental exercises.

Memory exercises can be valuable. The mental exercises of Zen and yoga can help. Teaching yourself new habits and eliminating bad ones is a powerful skill. What most of us need, however, is more skill in observing our own thinking. This is part of the great self-management skill called insight.

I enjoy repeating the conundrum: "Take time to think about how you are thinking about what you are thinking about." This is an enormously valuable skill for self-management in times of distress, conflict, and unusual opportunity; while others are in panic or slip into reactionary habits, a mentally fit pastor is able to understand what is going on and make realistic decisions.

NUTRITION

Nutrition for the brain or mind is receiving major attention in biochemical, molecular, and neurophysiological laboratories. It is becoming apparent that we can learn to enhance brain function through altering food and hydration habits. We can improve the management of cues and settings for enhanced thinking. We can even reprogram our minds and develop alternate styles of organizing and processing our thinking. (Several major magazines have featured essays on brain-mind research lately, which can be reviewed in the library. Also, look for literature by wise researchers such as Antonio Damasio, Richard Davidson, Michael Gazzaniga, Barbara Brown, and Robert Ornstein.)

COMPUTERS

Computers are becoming a metaphor and resource for understanding and enhancing mental functioning and fitness. If you use a computer, you have probably already appreciated this, for in testing our computer skills we see the importance of clear communication and of patient reprogramming, and we see the dangers of mental overload and clutter.

REST

Rest is another tool for managing our minds. The human brain never stops working, but it does function at differing levels of intensity. Training in biofeedback is where most of us learned about our ability to manage the mental intenseness (stress) of our brain waves. Being able to regulate our brain waves is a skill that increases our ability to manage our moods, creativity, and serenity; we now know that our minds can function effectively at a lower level of intensity than we thought. Being relaxed is not apathy or laziness, it is smart. We can improve our ability to rest and relax our minds quite easily, with some continuing education in biofeedback and meditation.

DEALING WITH ANGER

After these general insights regarding mental health, we turn to an important and specific factor related to conflict and abuse. It is anger—the displeasure reaction to injury and violation of personhood. Anger is discussed in general terms in Chapter 10. Here we examine it briefly as it relates to frustration and attack.

Anger is a natural, normal reaction to injury and attack. We do not have a choice about becoming angry when certain cues occur because anger is an automatic emotion. But we do have choices about which cues we will allow to anger us, and about how we will manage our anger. This is where self-awareness and mental health are relevant. People who do not have insight and mental discipline quickly become victims of their own reactions, as well as victims of the damage inflicted by others.

Anger ranges in intensity and involvement from simple irritation to out-of-control rage. Most of us limit ourselves to feeling irritation or a more intense outrage or sense of violation. Because anger is a primary (nonrational, dominant) emotion, it is difficult to think clearly or sensitively under its influence. Therefore, we must develop mental discipline before becoming angry in order to behave appropriately when we feel anger. Mental discipline includes awareness of anger, having an appropriate pattern of behavior ready for managing anger, and a mental assessment process by which we evaluate how well we manage the anger.

Being able to manage anger well in situations of intense emotional conflict is a most valuable skill and absolutely necessary for leaders. This management, however, does not include denying our anger or projecting it onto others. Rather, managing anger well means being conscious of the anger while retaining the ability to think well about what is going on. Managing anger also means using the energy from the anger (all emotions are energy) for managing the situation instead of dissipating it fruitlessly.

When a person's identity and integrity are injured or under attack, all kinds of responses are possible. It is natural to feel shock, pain, and confusion along with anger. But if these can be governed thoughtfully, it is possible to avoid deeper damage and to find creative ways to overcome the threat and pain. How we allow our minds to conceive of what is happening is all important. For example, if I begin to think of myself as a victim, I will soon develop victim-thinking. This means I will pity myself, I will blame someone, and I will seek vengeance or escape. But if I can learn to think like a survivor or a leader, I develop survivor-thinking and help others to do the same.

Mental discipline does not rely on magical thinking; it must be realistic. I must recognize my injury and acknowledge the related collateral damage. I must note the source of attack and I must assess realistically what I can do and what kind of help I need. In the same way, pastors and their intimates who are under attack develop creative strategies for making positive use of anger energy. This is what good spiritual leaders do. Part of this mental discipline is toughmindedness. For me, this term does not mean arrogance, abrasiveness, or insensitivity. It means rationality with soul and ego-strength. The soul is aware of the larger spiritual context for everything. The ego-strength is the personal, legitimized participation in what is happening. I can be toughminded, not because I know everything and am powerful, but rather because I am created in the image of God with a mission from God.

More specifically, toughmindedness for pastors is the ability to sort out issues and emotions and cut through to the truth, or at least the truth as I and the community of faith perceive it. It means I can see what is really going on, not just what people think is going on. I can see consequences, not just expectations. I can see authenticity, not just performances. I even have the ability, through the gift of discernment, to see the difference between good and evil.

In conflict and abuse situations, this toughmindedness gives me the confidence and courage to say, "Enough, already!" to abusers; to say, "This is evil, you cannot do this," to perpetrators; and to say "This is the way, walk in it" to confused believers (see Isaiah 30:21; John 14:6; and 1 Corinthians 12:31b).

But most important to me personally, such toughmindedness helps me put conflict and personal attacks and personal suffering in the larger perspective of God's purposes. I am much stronger than I sometimes think, especially when battered. But beyond my strength is the potential synergistic strength of the community of faith, and the promised strength of God whom I represent (Philippians 4:13).

It is the soft, fluffy, people-pleasing image of pastoring that has eroded our confidence in speaking the truth. Such softness makes me look like red meat to church predators. It is victim-thinking that robs me of this toughness, my ability to endure for God's purposes, and even my own integrity. Toughmindedness should not blind me to my own limits, or make toughness a macho goal. My source of strength is my faith in God (Ephesians 6:10).

Related to this toughmindedness is "command presence" which is often vital to leadership. Though this is a term I learned in military service, I am not advocating giving orders, macho dominance, or arrogance in pastoral ministry. I am talking about the often quiet confidence of wisdom and the visible authority of legitimate purpose. In a pastor, this command is apparent in physical posture, in direct eye contact, in nondefensiveness, in speaking with disciplined authority. Command presence says, "I know what I am doing" and "Don't mess with me!" The commanding presence of a pastor is like none other. It combines sensitivity, discernment, and the courage to speak for God. This representative, commanding presence is a natural development of a healthy body, mind, and spirit. It is not an ego trip or a manipulative performance. When you see it, you know.

FITNESS FOR THE SPIRIT

Fitness requires continuing education for the spirit as well as the mind and body. Spiritual fitness isn't automatic for clergy. In fact, we may have to work at it harder simply because it is crucial to our calling and because we can so easily "go through the motions" while losing the reality.

Fitness of the spirit has been receiving considerable attention in theology and pastoral psychotherapy in recent years. Because this is such an important part of our spiritual leadership and ministry, most of us have invested in it considerable continuing education time. We should continue, because our parishioners are yearning for spiritual experience and information, and some of them are gorging on spiritual junk food.

Systems theory has taught us that all members of an organization are interdependent and interactive, whether they recognize this or not. Therefore, it is difficult to have a healthy congregation without a healthy pastor, and vice versa, since ministry is most effective when it is a shared process. However, given the present condition of institutional religion, it is apparent that if the pastor does not lead the way and model spiritual fitness and ministry, it is unlikely that the lay leaders will be spiritually fit. A wise pastor will not only lead the way, she will also teach parishioners how to be spiritually fit and how to share the responsibility for spiritual leadership.

Wholeness, as presented in the Bible, includes the following principles:
Principle 1: Wholeness is a functional state of being. That is, it has a purpose—God's purpose. It is not simply a "feel good" condition for our comfort. Therefore, when we think of wholeness, we need to reprogram our thinking, for although physical comfort and pleasure can be included, wholeness is our intentional fulfilling of God's purpose. The root meaning of the Hebrew term for wholeness, *shalom,* is salvation and peace. Such wholeness is a resource as well as an experience. Therefore, we are responsible for the stewardship of it (see Isaiah 55:7–9, John 15:1–5).

Principle 2: Wholeness begins with spiritual health, which is union and communion with God, and all of creation; without God as our reference point, we will be limited to our own designs. This is what distinguishes the biblical view of wholeness from other perspectives on health. The medical model and its efforts to eliminate illness and physical disabilities has its limits. There are also limits to the psychological model and its efforts to eliminate bad thinking and behavior. There are even limits to the social model (for example, "The American Dream") and its goal of happiness for all. But wholeness includes an openness to the God beyond our limits (see Psalm 42:1–2 and Colossians 1:27).

Principle 3: Wholeness is an inclusive more than an individual experience. Though individuals may participate in wholeness, none are fully whole until all are whole. Moreover, wholeness is ecological; the interdependence of systems ties our condition and fate to that of the total creation (see Romans 8:19–23 and 1 Corinthians 12:12–26).

Principle 4: Wholeness is not perfection. Wholeness is big enough to include our pain, our mistakes, and the floundering of our healing and growth process. We participate in the benefits of wholeness whenever our beliefs, sensitivities, and practices are uniting with God's purposes. Thus, we may be in pain or comfort, error or goodness, and still share in the benefits of wholeness. Even our sin need not exclude us from wholeness, when we repent (see 2 Corinthians 12:7b–10).

Principle 5: Fulfilling God's purposes, which is crucial to wholeness, requires more than the potential for healing and growth that is built into our bodies, minds, and spirits. Our thinking—our "will," as some theologians call it—needs to be transformed from its natural self-centeredness. Traditions, habits, and misinformation limit our wholeness. The "anti-wholeness" of evil can delude or confuse us. Our minds and spirits are transformed, and we are opened to wholeness through a convergence of God's grace and our acceptance of this transforming grace. God offers wholeness but does not impose it. We must respond to God's offer positively lest we exclude ourselves from wholeness (see Isaiah 6:5–8 and Romans 12:1–2).

This view of health is valuable not only for what it teaches, but because it is biblical. Because the Bible is the primary reference, for Christians at least, this allows us to have a common reference point for our understanding and practice of fitness and health.

The five principles of biblical wholeness are relevant to the conflict and abuse occurring in many churches. They help us see not only what is sickness but how health is achieved. Principle 1, the functional principle, helps us see that health is built upon God's purposes, not our own. Principle 2, the spirituality principle, reminds us that budgets, programs, and rituals are important, but they can be unhealthy unless union and communion with God and creation is at the core. Principle 3, the inclusivity principle, helps us get past our self-centered and parochial perspectives on health. The fourth principle, the process principle, allows us to recognize various stages and conditions of health rather than bickering over who is and who isn't healthy. Principle 5, the transformation principle, teaches us that we all need transformation of various kinds in order to be forgiven, healed, and open to spiritual growth.

SPIRITUAL DISCIPLINES FOR SPIRITUAL FITNESS

The role of pastor is the oldest human profession of all, and the only one built upon spiritual experience and discernment. Constant temptations and pressures distract us. Therefore, there is no deep spiritual health for pastors, nor can they provide effective spiritual leadership without a consistent practice of the presence of God. The traditional name for this practice is "spiritual discipline." Though this term is not comfortable for all, it does name the key to spiritual growth and leadership. Other terms such as "piety" and "dedication" may be more helpful for some, but I prefer this nomenclature because it uses precise and simple names for the ingredients that make it work.

We all have a sense of what the words "spiritual" and "discipline" mean, even if our definitions vary somewhat. Though we have the image of God built into us, it does not flourish unless nourished and allowed to bear fruit. Spiritual disciplines are different than doing what comes naturally. Our natural tendencies are to seek comfort, pleasure, and adulation. As we mature, we learn that these lead to gratification but not to health. We also learn that to achieve a higher lifestyle than these, we must develop a health-oriented regimen in our lives. The benefits are health, fitness, and deep satisfactions and joys, rather than mere gratification. Most of us find that we must learn and relearn the value of spiritual disciplines since the seduction of gratifications is ever present.

In recent years, tools like the Food Guide Pyramid (mentioned earlier) have helped us develop a mental picture of the ingredients of healthy nutrition. Though this pyramid analogy is not a perfect one for spiritual disciplines, I find it useful in visualizing, evaluating, and adjusting my spiritual regimen. Perhaps it will be useful for you.

It should be obvious that each person must adapt these ingredients for his or her own spiritual health. If we continue to use the physical nutrition metaphor here, we also recognize that nutritional needs vary with activities, age, life stages, and other factors. Yet we recognize that without good nutrition, health deteriorates—inevitably. And without good health, functioning, mood, and perception also deteriorate. A person subjected to poor nutrition over a long period of time will not remain healthy.

Discipline sounds like a good idea to most of us, but it is also a forbidding word because it suggests discomfort, difficulty, and deprivation. When first begun or when done poorly, discipline is uncomfortable. But when a program of spiritual nutrition is followed healthfully as part of a realistic regimen, it becomes a comfortable and desirable way of life. Adjustments and adaptations will be necessary, of course, just as we eat more or less or change meal habits under different circumstances. Sometimes morning meditations are most nurturing, sometimes evening works best. Sometimes worship works best alone with God, sometimes with others, and so on.

PRAYER

Prayer is the primary spiritual discipline for most believers because it is most adaptable, most universal, and the simplest of the disciplines. I find that my personal practice of prayer has changed distinctly over the years. In my youth my prayers were essentially begging God for things and pleading for God to do certain things. As I've matured I find that my prayers are much more a listening-talking exchange. I spend more prayer time simply trying to open myself to discerning God's purposes and more time listening to the ineffable communications of God's Holy Spirit to my heart and mind.

Prayer is a very personal behavior for me. I find myself more and more reluctant to pray in public, except with those who are in dire need or who are praying in the same manner as I am. Public prayers often seem like a performance—perhaps helpful, but still only a performance.

Prayer is because I am. It is my personal soul in union and communion with God, with art, with quietness, with other people when they are allowing themselves to be authentic. Western religions that emphasize words tend to repel many, and Eastern mystical, meditative spiritual experiences attract many. The silence of Quaker (Friends) meetings is attractive and nurturing for this reason. Our noisy, wordy, exuberant Protestant worship services lose something vital because they seldom include quiet meditation. Only human voices are heard. The beautifully symbolic rituals can become performances.

We are all in the process of creating our God much of the time, not because we are intentionally idolatrous, but because no one has seen God. All our "revelations" are mediated through human images and experience. There is a real, true God, of course. Most of us are seeking and sometimes are in touch with this God. But because we are so visually and tactually oriented, we yearn for a God we can see and touch. It is natural then, when we cannot see or touch God, to create such experiences. This is a strong reason why we need the corrective of the community of faith, and the spiritual disciplines of discernment; the God I am creating can so easily be nothing more than what I want or need God to be, justified by whatever interpretation of Scripture verifies this need.

Again, my personal prayers become important because they mirror the kind of God I am creating. What kind of God am I projecting when I beg for what I want, when I plead my cause, when I call down fire from heaven on my enemies, when I strut my righteousness and my thoughts before God? Indeed, what is prayer—especially when I am battered, confused, and frightened? And what is God's part of my prayers when God is trying to speak to me in such conditions?

Physical prayer (posture, movement) is important to help me stay in touch with the sensual and symbolic nature of prayer. I find that my postures, my mental images acted out, symbolic rituals, touching and caressing, exercise and dance, and even immobility all add depth to prayer. More and more I find that they help me get in touch with spiritual energy and the rhythms of God's world and purposes. Physical prayer can be a recovering of ancient and revered regimens for spiritual nurture and guidance.

INGREDIENTS OF THE SPIRITUAL DISCIPLINES PYRAMID

The pyramid model, with its several ingredients, suggests that we make conscious selections, that some ingredients are needed in greater quantities than others, but that all are necessary to good nutrition. In other words, all ingredients are good, but moderation and need should determine choice.

Many fine resources exist for developing and evaluating spiritual disciplines. I do not propose a specific one, I only offer the reminder that Aunt Collie's truism applies to physical, mental, and spiritual health: "We get sick when we forget how to be well." After seeing hundreds of cases of serious conflict and clergy abuse, I believe nothing helps a hurting or wounded pastor more than spiritual health.

Just as the Food Guide Pyramid includes the basic ingredients in nutrition arranged in hierarchical form (the most important and most frequently needed ingredients are toward the bottom of the pyramid), the Spiritual Disciplines Pyramid has a similar arrangement. However, prayer is usually assumed to be the most important and frequently needed spiritual discipline. I agree. But for me the most important form of prayer is worship; therefore, it is at the base of the pyramid. Worship includes silence, praise, and individual as well as corporate communion with God. Worship becomes an attitude, sharpened and focused by liturgy and communal forms. When practiced continually, it becomes a lifestyle. This is not the same as self-righteousness, piousness, or empty habits. Rather, it is the sincere piety that can inform and guide the everyday life of any believer, in any circumstance—job, school, home, parish.

The prayer ingredient at the top of the Spiritual Disciplines Pyramid refers to private and public prayers of petition and intercession to liturgical prayer. They are obviously important, but are used less often and are less nurturing than the prayer attitude called worship in this pyramid.

The ingredients between worship and prayer are self-explanatory to pastors, with the possible exception of caring. Caring means love in action. This ingredient can easily be used to induce guilt trips in pastors, so we must remind ourselves that caring is a spiritual discipline, an activity we pursue in the right proportions to achieve good spiritual health. When we expect to care for everyone perfectly, or care beyond our healthy capacities, such caring is no longer a discipline.

Spiritual disciplines, like self-pastoring, require assistance from spiritually competent peers. We can and must do our own part in spiritual disciplines and accept primary responsibility for living spiritually disciplined lives. But we need the community of faith and professional peers to add the healthy ingredients we cannot fully provide ourselves. For example, it can be exceedingly helpful to have a competent spiritual director (confessor, spiritual friend, spiritual guide, mentor) who will accept responsibility to guide us in our practice of spiritual disciplines. Spiritual direction is already becoming something of a fad in some circles; therefore, discretion is important in considering this option. It is disturbing, on one hand, to see how quickly some organizations are competing to define and train people for the role of spiritual director. Excesses are possible. On the other hand, it is reassuring to see the growing legitimacy and use of this ancient role.

Just as the Food Guide Pyramid is intended to serve the general needs for physical health and must be adapted to needs and conditions, the Spiritual Disciplines Pyramid is intended to serve the needs for spiritual health. It is part of the long list of resources that provide spiritual health for pastors, and less vulnerability to clergy killers.

N O T E S

14

HEALTHY CONGREGATIONS

Healthy congregations are an enormous asset to all: the society, the community, the denomination, and the pastor. This book concludes with a vision of health—healthy congregations in general and healthy ways of understanding and managing sicknesses that occur in the church. Aunt Collie's "We get sick when we forget how to be well" applies to congregations as well as individuals. The clergy killer phenomenon is teaching us this truism over and over. (You may wish to review the previous chapter on clergy fitness as you read this chapter. It discusses the five principles of health and wholeness as the Bible presents them.)

The increase in health awareness in our society benefits organizations as well as individuals. We are beginning to realize that healthy organizations (families, neighborhoods, congregations) tend to produce healthy individuals, and vice versa. In fact, systems theory reminds us of the strong correlation between individual and organizational health.

Until recently, we typically did not think of congregations in terms of health; we have developed a habit of thinking about communities of faith in terms of demographics and logistics. This is useful for a CEO or stockholder in a business but it is not the stuff of mission and ministry, except as collateral information. It is easier to assess the sickness of a congregation through symptoms than to assess its health through numbers. Much like physicians, we have become specialists in seeing sickness and trying to cure it, rather than in seeing health and nurturing it.

Because we have become accustomed to looking for warning signals of sickness in congregations, it may be helpful to compile a list of the characteristics of health. These are not prioritized, since health can involve different combinations of these factors in diverse settings. Consider these signs:

➻ Infectious smiles, laughter, and celebration (not flippancy)
➻ A pandemic sense of reverence and respect (not piousness)
➻ A spreading witness to God's salvation (not parochial triumphalism)
➻ Fitness in organization and maintenance (not careless shabbiness)
➻ High levels of affirmation and recognition (not jealousy)
➻ Exploratory learning and programming (not stodginess)
➻ Allergic reactions to injustice (not a sense of entitlement)
➻ Quick recuperation from setbacks (not victim-thinking)
➻ Passionate stewardship (not possessiveness)
➻ Chronic interest in negotiating differences (not competitiveness)
➻ Persistent positive expectations (not complaining)
➻ Sensitivity to each other's needs (not exploitation)
➻ Efficacious care for pastors (not employer-employee attitudes)

The humorous overtones in this list are not intended as a cavalier approach to this crucial issue. Rather, the list is metaphorical in emphasizing that wellness can be as infectious and threatening to sickness, as sickness is to wellness.

The market is flooded with books on how to make a congregation grow. The ones I have read are useful. This chapter, however, is not about growing a congregation. In my experience, growth takes care of itself when a congregation is healthy spiritually, mentally, and physically. So I encourage pastors and congregants to spend a lot of time studying spiritual and mental fitness, and doing healthy things. When we have a clear picture of congregational wholeness and do healthy things, fitness is the result—and fitness is attractive, even contagious, to outsiders.

The market is also full of books by a new breed of "spirituality designers" who offer formulas, exercises, regimens, and such. Some of these are nurturing, but some may be spiritual junk food. (The apostle Paul spoke about the difference between milk and meat as spiritual nourishment. See 1 Corinthians 3:2.) As noted in the previous chapter, my approach is to encourage the practice of healthy spiritual disciplines and then let spiritual growth and innovation develop out of this lifestyle.

I have one other burden (spiritual reason) for writing about healthy congregations. I believe there is a glaring need for respect in our congregations and civility in our society. The church could be leading the way in meeting this need. Instead, many of our congregations are conflicted and insensitive. They are sick.

HEALTH IS A THREE-LETTER WORD

Three dynamics are characteristic of healthy congregations. They might seem rather obvious to thoughtful spiritual leaders, but studying them can stimulate creative answers to many of our questions about contemporary church conflicts. These are: worship, openness, and witness. After reducing my experience of healthy congregations to three descriptive words, I noted with amusement that taken together, the first letter in each of these words forms a word in itself—"wow." This three-letter word is a bit cute for my taste, but there may be some value in using it as an acronym, for it does express positive enthusiasm, and God knows we could use more of that in many of our congregations!

WORSHIP

The term "worship" is so familiar that we need to regularly reflect on its awesome meanings. I find it worthwhile to sit quietly, repeating a word like this and letting my mind do free association with it. (It may be useful here to review the discussion of worship in the previous chapter.) Besides our formal definitions of worship, we may say that worship is pausing to recognize that individually and together we belong to God. It doesn't work to say that God belongs to me or us. God is always a mystery, greater than anything we can imagine or create.

We have no choice but to let God be a mystery. Letting God be a mystery is the necessary humility with which we recognize our God. It is a valuable part of worship as well, for hubris is ever present in us ("I am proud of my humility!"). Moreover, this pride naturally leads to assumptions about God. One is that God simply must be like me in many ways. But beyond this is the primal process of creating God. We know better, at a conscious level. But at the deep unconscious level we yearn for and need God so acutely that we project our image into a virtual reality. Thus, God becomes whomever or whatever we need God to be. Such a god is too small (J. B. Phillips, *Your God Is Too Small* [New York: The Macmillan Co., 1957]). Worse, such a God is infinitely manipulable.

The up side is that God is far too great (*mysterium tremendum,* according to German theologian Rudolf Otto) to be only what I want God to be. And because God has identified Godself to us as affirming of us, we need not fear God as people have for centuries. Instead, we may confidently be intrigued and captivated in awe (*fascinans,* Otto), and even aspire to shared steward-ship of creation with God.

Let's apply our insights about worship to the concept of spiritual and emotional health. Health is a fragile gift. Even the heartiest of us can abuse and destroy it (Mickey Mantle, Jerry Garcia, you, and me). We must then come to think of health in the congregation not as a given but as potential, as stewardship of a functioning, living organism, the community of faith. (I pre-fer the analogy of a congregation as a living organism to the family analogy, because a congregation is far too diverse and large to function as a family.)

The Bible is full of examples of the potential for health being destroyed or enhanced, intentionally and unintentionally. Over and over, God gives Israel and individuals simple instructions on spiritual health (God's instructions to Adam and Eve in Eden, the Ten Commandments, Micah 6:8, the Sermon on the Mount). But turning these instructions into practice is enormously difficult. This is why humility is the beginning of health. I did not create it. I don't fully understand it. I can't even control it. I can only manage it—with God's help, and a little help from my friends.

Thus it is imperative to approach congregational health humbly. This, of course, is a major reason confession is featured in liturgy. It is important to me, not to God, to confess not only that I am a sinner but that I sin against my spiritual health and the health of this congregation. Toughest of all is naming my sins; for often I am in denial about them.

Now, worship flows from humility. We bow silently, wordlessly, because we don't even know what to say. Such worship begins to generate health. Now, instead of pretending I understand God or that I can assume and create my own spiritual health, I simply listen—for God. In listening, I open myself to communion with God, which is both worship and spiritual health.

Silence, listening for God, was not part of my religious tradition. I was taught to plead with God, to placate God, to congratulate myself with others for understanding God. It was while living in Asia that I encountered the concept of a God so big I could only worship and blend with God's purposes. Manipulation was out of the question.

Later in Quaker meetings, I experienced the silent expectancy of the community of faith. To sit silently, openly, together, waiting for a word from God, was a wakeup call for me. Even later, in silent retreats and free-form meditations, I learned and am learning the humility and quietness of worship.

Whenever I lead worship I am troubled by our compulsive need to do things, to say things, to control worship. Perhaps some of our sicknesses are thereby autogenic, that is, self-induced.

Silence—reflecting humility—is not the only cue for health. The spiritual joy of communion with God and with each other is an important ingredient. Just as endorphins (peptide hormones in the brain) help set up the circle of health in our minds, so the joyous experience of God helps set up the spiritual health circle in our hearts. Endorphins have the marvelous capacities to ease pain, give feelings of well-being and euphoria, facilitate the immune system in its fight against disease, and finally, to aid us in acting in healthful ways (for example, to think positively, desire proper nutrition and rest, and so forth), even when we don't especially feel healthy.

Along with humility and joy comes the management of our sacred symbols. We respond to sensual cues as human beings. Sight, sound, smell, touch, and taste, as well as intuition (sixth sense) stimulate our health. Without stimulation we wither and die. Healers and physicians know the value of symbols to health. Stethoscopes, pills, reassuring touch all trigger impressions of healing. We have such symbols in the church. Ours are naturally oriented to health more than sickness and healing, however, unless we turn them into instruments of sickness. We are touched by crosses, altars, chalices, vestments, organ, choir, smiles, handshakes, incense, even eating together. All these together promote spiritual health.

Finally, with worship comes reverence for life, for all of creation, and respect for each other as explicated by Martin Buber in his book *I-Thou* (New York: Charles Scribner's Sons, 1970). Albert Schweitzer and Martin Buber were my earliest instructors in the disciplines of reverence and respect. More recently, Martin Luther King Jr., Jeremy Rifkin, Matthew Fox, Robert Bellah, and many others are helping me remember what Jesus taught so long ago. Such respect for life in all its forms is a deterrent to violence and abuse.

OPENNESS

Openness is the second dynamic notable in a healthy congregation. We can treat this dynamic more briefly, not because it is less important but because it is less complex. Openness as used here means a natural readiness to listen to other people and perspectives, and to seek out information and creative options from others within and outside the community of faith. Openness means less parochialism and less defensiveness.

Research on congregations shows that openness is reflected in hospitality, acceptance of diversity, and in an active dialogue on issues important to the world, as well as to the community of faith. Such openness is both a reflection and a facilitator of congregational health. People and organizations open to the outside use less energy in defensiveness, more effectively communicate and care for each other, and typically generate more financial, volunteer, and prayer support for worthwhile missions and causes. Moreover, they are more likely to have a positive reputation in the community.

It should also be apparent that when openness is present in a community of faith, members are not only open to each other and the outside community, they are more open to the leading of God's Holy Spirit, even when God leads in new directions. The apostle Paul learned to be open the hard way, on the road to Damascus (Acts 9) and through a "thorn in the flesh" (2 Corinthians 12). Openness is not an automatic human characteristic and skill. It must be learned through spiritual disciplines, as is true of all three of these health dynamics.

WITNESS

The third congregational health dynamic is witness. Though this also sounds like a familiar term, its contemporary meanings combine the best of traditional and new insights.

"Witness" here means both the testimonials to what God is doing in individual and parish life and the witness to Jesus' example through the good works he would likely do now if he were physically present. There is no agreement on all aspects of witness. But few believers are against witnessing about our faith.

Witness is a sign of health and an inducement to health. When our communion with God is alive and well within us we cannot help but tell about it. The fact of sharing spiritual health with others through testimonial and active caring nurtures such health, besides passing it on to others.

I am not advocating the judgmental triumphalism of arrogant faith. Rather, recognizing that just as physical and mental health are visible and express themselves in healthy sharing, so does spiritual health. Witnessing includes the creative search for what could be, as well as affirming what already is true in our experience. It includes having the spiritually healthy members standing up for righteousness when evil threatens.

OTHER CHARACTERISTICS OF HEALTH

Several useful books have been written on the subject. Two that I have found helpful are Kennon L. Callahan's *Twelve Keys to an Effective Church* (San Francisco: Harper San Francisco, 1983) and Robert Wuthnow's *Christianity in the Twenty-first Century* (New York: Oxford University Press, 1993). From my own research and experience, I list the characteristics of congregational health most pertinent to the subject of this book. This list is not arranged in order of importance. Each is important in its own way.

RESPECT FOR PASTOR

Spiritual leadership roles are respected in the congregation, especially the role of pastor. This characteristic was discussed in a previous chapter but needs to be included here.

Respect does not mean putting the pastor on a pedestal. Nor does it mean that what the pastor does is above review and accountability. It does mean that the reverence for God is extended to the role of the pastor as a representative of God. The pastor represents several spiritual entities beyond herself: God, the community of faith, and religious faith in the everyday life of the society. Because he represents such entities does not mean he is infallible or without human sin. Rather, it means people continue to need a reminder of that which is greater than themselves (God, the community of faith, creation), and guidance in living their beliefs—from a person who devotes his life to such matters.

This is a traditional view of the pastoral role, of course. In recent years it has been questioned, even discarded. My point is that without this respected and healthy role, the church tends to flounder and the community loses a salutary presence.

EFFECTIVE GRIEVANCE PROCESS

Without a simple, effective grievance process, any complaint in the congregation can be a threat to the health, peace, and unity of the congregation. Further, without a legitimate and widely known grievance procedure, many complaints eventually land on the pastor's desk. Then it is easy for complaints to become criticism of the pastor.

Given that most denominational polities and congregational bylaws contain at least a rudimentary method for handling conflict, it is surprising how few pastors and elected leaders use it, and how few parishioners know about it. When there is no grievance process or it is not widely known, conflict is reduced to the animal level—the law of the jungle. When there is a grievance procedure, it must be understood, publicized, and invoked in order for it to be effective. And when it is invoked, most complainants, concerns, and questions can be handled without inflaming the whole congregation, draining leadership energies, and eroding the mission of the church.

Some people wonder whether publicizing the grievance procedure will encourage more complaints. This is similar to the argument that sex education produces more sexual behavior. Complaints, concerns, and questions, however, are a natural part of any human organization. Awareness of how to manage them may produce a few more complaints, but it is more likely that awareness will reassure people that there really is a legitimate, peaceful way to handle such matters. Without a known and used grievance process, these matters tend to incubate underground.

An official grievance process needs to be simple. Typically a specific person is identified as the initial contact. This person is an officially elected and publicly accountable person. The process includes a sensitive procedure for bringing the complaint to the officially elected board, which will determine the problem's resolution. Next, the process requires a clear reporting of action to the complainant. The process needs to have teeth—enforcement sanctions. And, there needs to be a court of appeals in case complications arise that are not manageable at the board level.

HEALING

Healing is another necessary characteristic of healthy congregations since sickness, injury, and disability are real possibilities even in the presence of health. (Note the principle of inclusion discussed as an aspect of biblical wholeness.)

In recent years the church has tended to turn healing over to the medical and mental health professions. They provide significant help, of course. But it has again become evident that spirituality and religious faith are prime ingredients in healing and health. It is reassuring to see the resurgence of interest and actual practice of healing in congregations. This opens the church to some influence of fads and charlatans, as we know. But that is a good reason for legitimate teaching and practice of healing in the church.

Healthy congregations recognize the reality of sickness in body, mind, and spirit. They do what is possible with their resources to meet needs for healing. They must recognize their limits and use outside resources as well, but they express concern and active involvement for those who are suffering and they keep the pursuit of wholeness active in the congregation.

Preaching and teaching on sickness and health will occur regularly in a health-oriented congregation. Regular healing services need to be conducted in spiritually competent ways. Support groups should be formed for suffering people, for those who care for such people, and for all who wish to learn more about human health and sickness. For those who need help outside the church, referral lists should be available. Finally, emphasis must be placed on the physical, mental, and spiritual disciplines needed to maintain health and treat illness.

A healthy perspective in congregations now includes awareness, concern, and active stewardship of wholeness throughout our ecology and the full human family. The corporate principle of biblical wholeness teaches that none of us is truly healthy until all are.

CELEBRATION

Celebration is another characteristic of healthy congregations. When I visit congregations with which I am unfamiliar, I like to look at a recent copy of the Sunday bulletin and a current issue of the newsletter to see how affirmation and celebration is taking place. Everything from mentioning birthdays to appreciation for achievements to announcements of special celebratory events lifts the spirits of the congregation.

Humor, dance, enthusiastic music, joyful appreciation of the arts, storytelling, exuberant fun, and other positive interactions add "endorphins" to congregational life. Research and anecdotal data confirms the value of celebration in congregational life. Such joy leaves less room for anxiety, criticism, and conflict.

HEALTHY MODELS AND MENTORS

The modeling and mentoring of health is conspicuous in healthy congregations. Healthy congregations need people who are aware of the importance of living their faith, and of mentoring the weak and the young.

In the earlier discussion of the agendas of human behavior, the point was made that love is not an automatic human motivation. We are born only with the potential for love. In order for this potential to become healthy love in all its forms, children and people without legitimate love in their lives need to experience the feeling of being loved and to see love in action. Without such healthy models and mentoring, the potential for love and the yearning for love may become distorted by the unhealthy models and mentoring which are now so available in our society.

A HEALTHY VIEW OF DEATH AND THE DYING PROCESS

Sixth on this list is the ability to deal with death and dying. Organized religion always includes teachings and rituals related to death, of course. But in spite of the Bible's teachings about death it remains a frightening and conflicted issue for many. Healthy congregations deal with such matters openly and with hopeful trust. They discuss death openly and without fear. They teach and believe that death is a transition to a better life, not the end. And they cry together and console each other about losing people who are precious. Then they get on with healthy living.

Space is inadequate here for the needed reexamination of the accumulated distortions in the church and in society surrounding the experience of dying and death. Though our traditional religion teaches that death has been conquered and is only a transition to a better life, our real beliefs betray us and fear and grief pervade the typical experience of death and funerals in many congregations. Often, after a brief expression of consolation, the congregation and pastor leave those who have been deeply hurt by the loss to suffer in silence without the needed assistance in regaining health.

The unknowns of the death experience, the pain that accompanies some deaths, and the dreadful feelings of loss and unfairness tend to overshadow the positive, even joyful messages about death that the Bible and theology offer. Healthy death is not an oxymoron, it is only an enigma. We do not understand all we wish to know. But if any message is loud and clear, especially in the Newer Testament, it is that Jesus has preceded us on the path of death, and the inevitable outcome is resurrection to a much better life. It takes some serious study, spiritual disciplines, and caring interactions for a congregation to reverse the unhealthy distortions in contemporary understandings of death. But healthy congregations are finding ways to do this.

RESPECT FOR LAY LEADERS

Finally, it is important to remember that an important sign of congregational health is its treatment of its pastoral and lay leaders. The growing sickness among us tends to vent the frustration, pain, and confusion in contemporary society on moral and spiritual leaders. Healthy congregations are on the watch for such signs of spiritual sickness, and seek to surround and detoxify it with health.

God offers us the possibility of healthy congregations and healthy spiritual leaders, but it is up to us to accept and live this possibility because it is not automatic.

It makes sense to close this book with an emphasis on health and wholeness. We have identified a spiritual sickness exhibited by people called clergy killers. We have discussed how this sickness relates to conflict in the church and offered methods for managing these. But finally we must focus on health—physical, mental, and spiritual. We call this wholeness in the church. It is the vision that guides our mission and it is also the basic dynamic of healing and prevention in the face of the clergy killer phenomenon.

N O T E S

NOTES

ENERGY MANAGEMENT INVENTORY

The tree is a metaphor for management of personal energy resources. It is a living organism with a number of characteristics:

1. It has root and leaf systems that generate energy effectively.
2. Energy in must equal energy out.
3. The size and contribution of the tree depend upon the health of its life-support abilities and environment.
4. The tree is part of an ecological system and cannot exist in isolation.

All of our relationships (family, professional, and so forth) drain or restore energy. When energy systems

EXERCISE

On the branches of this tree, list the tasks and relationships that require energy from you.

Then qualify (1 to 10) the energy drain of each task and relationship.

Add the total and place it in the blank:

Energy Drainers

_____
(for a typical week)

Extra Drainers

_____
(this week)

Total _____

Energy exists in various forms and quantities. The physical, intellectual, emotional, and spiritual appartatus that generates our personal energy is limited. We cannot manufacture energy without resources and systemic health. Because the environment and the system change over time, the ability to adapt is crucial.

Any change—good as well as bad—uses energy. Crises and persistent stress not only use energy, but they also strain and may damage the energy system.

Paying attention to the management of our energy system is not selfishness, it is _good stewardship._

Notice that appratuch and relation

Write a brief description of your philosophy for managing your individual energy system.

_____
_____
_____
_____
_____

Is it effective? Why or why not?

_____
_____
_____
_____

On the roots of this tree, list the activities and relationships that give you energy.
Then qualify (1 to 10) the energy drain of each task and relationship. Add the total and place it in the blank:

Energy Enhancers

_____
(for a typical week)

Extra Enhancers

_____
(this week)

Total _____

List unusual energy drainers or enhancers in your life this week; and add them to the total.

Drainers

_____
_____
_____
_____

Total _____

Enhancers

_____
_____
_____
_____

Total _____

Does Your Present Life, Work, and Relationship Environment Provide Energy Balance?

SUPPORTIVE RELATIONSHIP INVENTORY

A support system is the cluster of people, experiences, and objects that allow me to live as I now do, and helps me grow. The absence of any one of these would change my life significantly and painfully.

Supportive relationships have always been foundational in a person's individual support system. But the mystique of the clergy role emphasizes self-sufficiency and a loner style. Therefore, intimacy requires resolve.

The half-intimacies of the pastoral role limit support further because pastors are expected to understand and support others without receiving intimacy in return. From such relationships the pastor receives the satisfaction of faithful caring and pleasure when these efforts are applauded. However, even though the pastor's need for two-way intimacy is legitimate, it is usually counterproductive to expect to have this need satisfied in professional relationships. The loneliness of spiritual leadership and the energy drain of dedicated caring produce a deficit that only intimate support can fill. God's presence is certainly supportive. Denominations may provide supportive resources. A person's own self-esteem is a requisite, also. But most of us need people to notice, care, and support us.

You may or may not understand your support system very well. The following brief inventory can clarify your support. Fill in the blanks preceding the support ingredients with names and experiences that provide support now. In the blanks following each ingredient, write in what is missing.

NOW	SUPPORT INGREDIENTS	NEEDED
	S—Services *(make supportive resources available)*	
	U—Undergirding *(realistic benefits)*	
	P—Political advocacy *(realistic protection)*	
	P—Peer relations *(nurturing relationships)*	
	O—Opportunity *(creativity and achievement)*	
	R—Respect *(positive image and integrity)*	
	T—Training *(learning, excellence)*	

SELECTED BIBLIOGRAPHY

Augsburger, David. *Conflict Mediation Across Cultures.* Louisville: Westminster/ John Knox Press, 1992.

Barna, George. *Today's Pastors.* Ventura, CA: Regal Books, 1993.

Clinebell, Howard. *Well Being.* San Francisco: Harper San Francisco, 1992.

Dossey, Larry. *Prayer Is Good Medicine.* San Francisco: HarperCollins, 1996.

Farley, Edward. *Good & Evil.* Minneapolis: Fortress Press, 1990.

Foster, Richard J. *Celebration of Discipline.* New York: Harper & Row, Publishers, 1978.

Gilbert, Barbara G. *Who Ministers to Ministers?* Washington, D.C.: The Alban Institute, 1987.

Glasser, William. *The Identity Society.* New York: Harper & Row, Publishers, 1972.

Halverstadt, Hugh. *Managing Church Conflicts.* Louisville: Westminster/John Knox Press, 1991.

Hands, Donald and Fehr, Wayne. *Spiritual Wholeness for Clergy.* Washington, D.C.: The Alban Institute, 1993.

Harbaugh, Gary L. *Pastor as Person.* Minneapolis: Augsburg Publishing House, 1984.

Haugk, Kenneth. *Antagonists in the Church.* Minneapolis: Augsburg Fortress Press, 1988.

Holmes, Urban T. *Spirituality for Ministry.* San Francisco: Harper & Row, Publishers, 1982.

Hunter, Rodney J., ed. *Dictionary of Pastoral Care and Counseling.* Nashville: Abingdon Press, 1990.

Johnson, Barry. *Polarity Management.* Amherst, MA: The HRD Press, Inc., 1992.

Johnson, David and VanVonderen, Jeff. *The Subtle Power of Spiritual Abuse.* Minneapolis: Bethany House Publishers, 1991.

Johnson, Vernon. *Intervention.* Minneapolis: Johnson Institute Books, 1986.

Kelsey, Morton. *Healing and Christianity.* Minneapolis: Augsburg Publishing House, 1995.

Leas, Speed. *Moving Your Church Through Conflict.* Washington D.C.: The Alban Institute, 1992.

Levin, Edward. *Negotiating Tactics: Bargain Your Way to Winning.* New York: Fawcett Columbine, 1980.

London, H. B. Jr. and Wiseman, Neil B. *Pastors At Risk.* Wheaton, IL: Victor Books/Sp Publications, Inc., 1993.

Maloney, H. Newton and Hunt, Richard A. *The Psychology of Clergy.* Harrisburg, PA: Morehouse Publishing, 1991.

Marney, Carlyle. *Priests to Each Other.* Valley Forge, PA: Judson Press, 1974.

McBurney, Louis. *Every Pastor Needs a Pastor.* Waco, TX: Word Books, 1977.

Moe, Kenneth Alan. *The Pastor's Survival Manual.* Bethesda, MD: The Alban Institute, 1995.

Neff, Pauline. *Tough Love.* Nashville: Abingdon Press, 1982.

Nelson, James B. *Embodiment.* Minneapolis: Augsburg Publishing House, 1978.

Nouwen, Henri J. M. *The Wounded Healer.* New York: Doubleday, 1972.

Oates, Wayne. *The Care of Troublesome People.* Bethesda, MD: The Alban Institute, 1994.

Oswald, Roy M. *How to Build a Support System for Your Ministry.* Washington D.C.: The Alban Institute, 1991.

Peck, M. Scott. *People of the Lie.* New York: Simon and Schuster, Inc., 1983.

Phillips, J. B. *Your God Is Too Small.* New York: The Macmillan Co., 1957.

Qualben, James. *Peace in the Parish.* San Antonio: Langmarc Publishing, 1991.

Rediger, G. Lloyd. *Coping with Clergy Burnout.* Valley Forge, PA: Judson Press, 1982.

_____. *Ministry and Sexuality: Cases, Counseling and Care.* Minneapolis: Fortress Press, 1990.

Roberts, Wes. *Support Your Local Pastor.* Colorado Springs, CO: NavPress, 1995.

Vaux, Kenneth L. *Health & Medicine in the Reformed Tradition.* New York: Crossroads Publishing Co., 1984.

Vickery, Donald M. and Fries, James F., eds. *Taking Care of Yourself.* New York: Addison-Wesley Publishing Co., 1994.

Wink, Walter. *Engaging the Powers.* Minneapolis: Fortress Press, 1992.